CULTURES OF THE WORLD
New Zealand

Cavendish
Square
New York

Published in 2018 by Cavendish Square Publishing, LLC
243 5th Avenue, Suite 136, New York, NY 10016
Copyright © 2018 by Cavendish Square Publishing, LLC

Third Edition

Library of Congress Cataloging-in-Publication Data

Names: Smelt, Roselynn, author. | Yong, Jui Lin, author. | Newsome, Joel, 1984- author.
Title: New Zealand / Roselynn Smelt, Yong Jui Lin, and Joel Newsome.
Description: New York : Cavendish Square, 2018. | Series: Cultures of the world | Includes bibliographical references and index.
Identifiers: LCCN 2017059330 (print) | LCCN 2017060078 (ebook) | ISBN 9781502636294 (eBook) | ISBN 9781502636287 (library bound)
Subjects: LCSH: New Zealand--Juvenile literature. | New Zealand--Description and travel--Juvenile literature.
Classification: LCC DU408 (ebook) | LCC DU408 .S563 2018 (print) | DDC 993--dc23
LC record available at https://lccn.loc.gov/2017059330

Editorial Director: David McNamara
Editor: Kristen Susienka
Copy Editor: Nathan Heidelberger
Associate Art Director: Amy Greenan
Designer: Alan Sliwinski
Production Coordinator: Karol Szymczuk
Photo Research: J8 Media

PICTURE CREDITS

Printed in the United States of America

CONTENTS

NEW ZEALAND TODAY

WITH ITS BREATHTAKING LANDSCAPES, SPELLBINDING wildlife, and unique culture, New Zealand has captured the imagination of citizens and visitors alike over the course of its relatively short history. The nation is home to two main cultures: the Maori (inhabitants of Polynesian descent whose presence in New Zealand dates back to about one thousand years ago) and the pakeha (New Zealanders of European descent who began arriving in the early 1800s). In the country's formative years, conflict arose when British colonizers arrived in droves, plummeting the native population through the introduction of foreign diseases, alcohol, and firearms. Though the nation's beginnings are fraught with conflict, New Zealand has developed into a strong, confident, and conscientious participant on the world stage.

New Zealand was the last significant landmass to be inhabited by man, and the culture reflects a forward-thinking populace. The country was the first to legalize women's suffrage, remains completely free of nuclear power, and in 2016 New Zealand was considered the least corrupt nation in the world (tied with Denmark), according to the Corruption Perceptions Index. While the country's colonial ties to

GEOGRAPHY

Lakes Rotoaira (*foreground*) and Taupo (*background*) are two of New Zealand's many natural wonders.

1

N EW ZEALAND'S NATURAL BEAUTY IS one of the island nation's chief points of pride. Located in the southwest Pacific Ocean, New Zealand enjoys a wealth of astonishing landforms. The landscape vacillates between mountains, glaciers, fjords, volcanoes, subtropical forests, and beaches. With the countryside offering this much diversity, it's no wonder New Zealand has become an increasingly popular destination for filmmaking.

Australia is New Zealand's closest neighbor. It lies 1,250 miles (2,011 km) northwest across the Tasman Sea. Antarctica is second closest. It sits just 1,400 miles (2,253 km) to the south. New Zealand's two major landmasses are the North and South Islands. They are separated by the Cook Strait, which is around 14 miles (23 km) at its narrowest width. South Island is the island nation's largest landmass and the twelfth-largest island in the world. The country also consists of many smaller islands, including Stewart Island and the Chatham Islands. According to the Central Intelligence Agency World Factbook, the total land area is 102,138 square miles (264,537 square kilometers), approaching the size of Colorado. New Zealand's islands are slim. The country stretches 1,000 miles (1,609 km) from north to south and spans about 280 miles (450 km) across. This long coastline lies between subtropical waters to the north and the sub-Antarctic Ocean to the south. With a

The Canterbury Plains feature some of the country's most prized farming landscape.

There are at least twenty large lakes in New Zealand and many smaller ones. Lake Taupo in the central North Island is the largest, with a surface area of 234 square miles (606 sq km). It was formed by an enormous volcanic eruption in 186 CE, during which an incredible 3,600 cubic miles (15,000 cubic km) of ash and pumice fell virtually all over the North Island.

The magnificent alpine settings and large lakes in the southwestern region of the South Island attract many visitors. Some artificial lakes have been created on both the North and South Islands to service hydroelectric projects. Numerous rivers speed their way down from the mountains to the sea. Because they flow so fast, they have become an important source of hydroelectric power. The longest river is the Waikato on the North Island, which flows 264 miles (425 km) into the Tasman Sea.

RICH SOIL

The most extensive flat area in New Zealand, the Canterbury Plains, lies along the eastern coast of the South Island. This is one of the richest farming areas because the soil is the result of millions of years of glacial deposits. Farms here are the country's main suppliers of wheat and grain, while the many sheep farms have made the area famous for "Canterbury Lamb" (New Zealand lamb that is exported—either chilled or frozen). There are also coastal plains in the Southland and Otago provinces. A number of coastal plains are found in the North Island: the Bay of Plenty produces dairy cattle, seafood, and a wide range of subtropical crops, while East Cape produces the bulk of the country's corn. East Cape, Hawke's Bay, and Marlborough in the South Island all have vineyards and fruit orchards.

HEAT BENEATH THE SURFACE

From the south of Lake Taupo to White Island, an active volcano in the Bay of Plenty, is a belt of geysers, boiling mud pools, and hot-water springs. One of these, Frying Pan Lake, is one of the world's largest hot springs. The lake has a surface area of 45,450 square yards (38,000 square meters). It is typically between 113 and 131 degrees Fahrenheit (45 to 55 degrees Celsius), but at its deepest point the temperature reaches 389°F (198°C). It also emits carbon dioxide and hydrogen sulfide—making the lake have an eerie, fog-like quality. Much of the country's thermal activity takes place in and around the city of Rotorua on the central North Island, located on the banks of the southern shore of Lake Rotorua.

Geothermal energy heats Frying Pan Lake.

Only four other countries have geysers—Iceland, Russia, Chile, and the United States. Geysers occur in areas where water from lakes and rivers seeps down into concentrations of hot rock, heats up rapidly in a confined space, and then explodes up through vents, emitting boiling water and steam. The water expelled by the geysers contains dissolved minerals that solidify into colorful and shapely silica formations on nearby surfaces as the water evaporates. It is claimed that the minerals in thermal waters are beneficial to human health. Rotorua has been a therapeutic bathing center of international repute since the late nineteenth century.

WEATHER

New Zealand's ocean environment keeps the climate mild, but the mountains, together with the prevailing westerly winds, cause marked differences in temperature and rainfall from west to east. This is particularly so in the South Island, where westerly winds cause the clouds to draw moisture from the sea. As they rise, the clouds hit the mountains, and rain is released onto the west coast. Fiordland is one of the wettest areas in the world. Drought often occurs on the east coast of both islands in summer (December—February). However, there is usually plenty of rain throughout the country, with winter (June—August) being the wettest season in the North Island and spring (September—November) being the wettest season on the South Island's west coast. The provinces of Auckland and Northland enjoy a year-round subtropical climate where citrus fruit is grown.

Mean annual temperatures range from 61°F (16°C) in Northland to 50°F (10°C) in the southernmost part of the country. The highest temperatures occur east of the mountain ranges in summer, creating hot and dry conditions, while the lowest temperatures occur during winter in the mountains and in the inland areas of Canterbury and Otago. There are few places where temperatures higher than 86°F (30°C) or lower than 14°F (−10°C) occur. Snow falls mainly in the mountains, but during the coldest month of the year (July), snow often falls for a few days in the eastern coastal provinces of the South Island.

WILDLIFE

Before New Zealand was inhabited by people, the land was covered in forest and "bush" (evergreen broadleaf trees and enormous tree ferns, ground ferns, and clinging vines). In the forests, native trees such as rimu (ri-moo), totara (TOR-tah-rah), and kauri (kah-oo-ree) grew to spectacular heights.

When the Maori people came to New Zealand from eastern Polynesia in the thirteenth century CE, they cleared one-third of the forests, and later (in the early nineteenth century), the European settlers cleared another third. Today, about 39 percent of New Zealand is covered in forest. Tree species in these areas include radiata pine, elm, birch, poplar, macrocarpa, and beech.

Coastal wetlands have other forms of native vegetation, as well as marine birds such as oystercatchers and migratory waders. Mangrove trees grow in swamps, mudflats, estuaries, and tidal creeks in Northland. New Zealand shrubland contains the highest proportion of tree-sized daisies and plants

MOA

The moa has an important place in New Zealand's history. Nine species of this flightless bird were endemic to the island nation when Polynesian settlers arrived. It is estimated that there were around fifty-eight thousand moa roaming New Zealand when humans arrived, and their numbers were thought to be increasing.

Unfortunately, the arrival of the Maori signaled the beginning of the end for the moa. Generations of Maori hunted the large birds for food and cleared the forests where the moas lived.

Some believe the moas went extinct in the sixteenth or seventeenth century, though other researchers suggest they might have gone extinct much sooner after the arrival of the Maori. While modern scientists were never able to directly observe the moas, information about their diet, reproduction, and physicality has been deduced as a result of fossil evidence and DNA samples. Several tracks of fossilized moa footprints have also been discovered. Their analysis has led scientists to believe they walked at speeds ranging from 1 to 3 miles per hour (1.6 to 4.8 kilometers per hour). They are thought to have eaten a wide variety of plant materials, including low-hanging leaves and fibrous twigs. The ancient birds swallowed stones that they held in their gizzards. These gizzard stones allowed them to grind coarse plant material that otherwise would have been impossible to digest.

Based on fossil and DNA evidence, it is believed that the moa took approximately ten years to reach adulthood. Materials at preserved nesting sites suggest that the nesting period for the moa was sometime in the late spring to early summer. Dozens of whole moa eggs have been preserved and are on display in museums. These eggs vary greatly in size, from around 5 inches to 9.5 inches (12.7 to 24.1 centimeters) long and around 4 inches to 7 inches (10.2 to 17.8 cm) wide.

While the various species of moa ranged in size, it is estimated that the largest species stood about 12 feet (3.7 m) high with their necks outstretched and weighed over 500 pounds (227 kilograms).

Despite previous speculation that a climatic event could have been responsible for the moas' demise, all scientific investigation has pointed to humans as the sole predators and ultimate drivers of moa extinction.

with interlocking and twisted branches in the world. In the grasslands, toetoe, pampas, and flax plants can be found. These were cultivated by the early Maori and were used to make baskets and clothing, thatching for houses, and ropes, sails, and rigging for ships.

Because New Zealand was cut off from the rest of the world by its oceans over eighty million years ago, only mammals that could fly were able to reach it. The only native land mammal in New Zealand is the bat. Other land mammals were introduced by the Maori and European settlers.

The vast majority of New Zealand's native species of reptiles and amphibians live only here and nowhere else in the world. New Zealand's native frogs lay eggs that turn into frogs within the frog egg. They do not have a free-swimming tadpole stage like other frogs do. They have tail-wagging muscles, but no tails. They do not croak like normal frogs do. Instead, they let out a thin, high-pitched squeak. They are among the world's most ancient frogs.

In the absence of other mammals and many predators, birdlife in New Zealand was, and still is, amazing. New Zealand is an avian wonderland, with many species evolving to take over niches that would normally be occupied by mammals.

The tuatara (too-uh-tah-ruh) is the largest reptile in New Zealand, growing up to 1.6 feet (0.5 m) long. It is the only surviving species of a family of reptiles that became extinct in other parts of the world sixty million years ago. Found only on New Zealand's offshore islands, the tuatara (which resembles an iguana) has traces of what was once a third eye. Tuataras are aggressive predators, ambushing their prey with spectacular bursts of speed and strength. They are one of the rarest reptiles on Earth.

An even more ancient "living fossil" is New Zealand's weta (we-tah), a giant wingless insect resembling a grasshopper (although it can't jump). It has hardly changed at all over the last 190 million years. The harmless weta is the heaviest insect in the world, weighing up to 2.5 ounces (71 grams). Its name means "god of ugly things." Like some insects, the weta breathes through its exoskeleton. Interestingly, it also has ears on its knees.

New Zealand also has one of the world's largest gecko lizards, Duvaucel's gecko (*H. duvaucelii*). New Zealand geckos are unusual because they give birth

With the incredible biodiversity of New Zealand, the kiwi stands out as one of the most recognizable symbols of New Zealand culture. They are so intrinsically linked with the island nation that New Zealanders are commonly referred to as "Kiwis." The nocturnal, flightless bird has a unique, long, slender bill with nostrils at the tip. Depending on the species, kiwis can stand anywhere from 10 to 20 inches (25 to 51 cm) tall and weigh anywhere from 3 to 7 pounds (1.4 to 3.2 kg).

Kiwis lay only one egg at a time. In relation to the bird's body size, the kiwi's egg is the largest in the world, weighing approximately one-third of the female bird's weight. After the egg is laid, male kiwi partners incubate and rear the young in most species.

The kiwi has an incredibly keen sense of smell, an unusual quality in birds. The kiwi sense of smell allows it to locate insects underground without seeing or feeling them. They eat seeds, grubs, worms, fruit, small crayfish, eels, and a variety of amphibians.

Once two kiwis have bonded, they are likely to remain a monogamous couple for life.

to live young—usually twins—rather than laying eggs. The only other geckos that do this live in New Caledonia (an island situated 1,056 miles [1,700 km] from New Zealand). The oldest wild Duvaucel's gecko lived to thirty-six years, but they can live to over fifty years in captivity.

URBAN AREAS

When the European settlers came to New Zealand in the early nineteenth century, they settled mainly in the South Island. But for the last one hundred years, people have been drifting north, and now a little over 3.67 million people (77 percent of the population) live in the North Island, with most of the population concentrated in the provinces of Northland, Auckland, Waikato, and Bay of Plenty, where the climate is warmer.

There are four main urban centers in New Zealand: Auckland and Wellington in the North Island and Christchurch and Dunedin in the South Island.

AUCKLAND is New Zealand's largest urban area. It occupies the isthmus between the Hauraki Gulf on the east coast and the Manukau Harbor on the west coast. With about one boat for every four households, Auckland has earned the name "City of Sails." A city of more than 1.5 million inhabitants, it is the most cosmopolitan place in the country and is the main tourist and trade gateway.

WELLINGTON, the capital of New Zealand, is located near the southern end of the North Island. It is the second-largest urban area, with a population of 496,000. Wellington Harbor, also called Port Nicholson, covers 31 square miles (80 sq km) and is considered one of the finest natural harbors in the world.

Auckland is New Zealand's most populated city and offers an impressive urban skyline.

CHRISTCHURCH is situated on the Canterbury Plains. It has a population of about 381,500. Early English settlers were successful in recreating an English society here. This is reflected in the city's English layout.

DUNEDIN has a population of about 127,000 and is located at the top of the long, fjord-like Otago Harbor. Settled originally by people from Scotland, Dunedin was named after the old Celtic name of Edinburgh, Dun Edin. It is sometimes called the Edinburgh of the South. It is here that New Zealand's only whiskey is distilled.

Dunedin is a large city with Scottish and Maori roots.

INTERNET LINKS

http://www.nationalgeographic.com/adventure/destinations/ oceania/new-zealand/21-spectacular-adventure-photos
This photo essay features twenty-one images showcasing New Zealand's majestic beauty.

https://www.nzgeo.com
Watch videos, read articles, and view images of New Zealand's beauty at *New Zealand Geographic* magazine's website.

HISTORY

The Maori arrived in New Zealand several hundred years before the Europeans.

2

NEW ZEALAND IS A YOUNG NATION IN terms of its position on the geological timeline and its populace. Because of its relative isolation, New Zealand is one of the last significant landmasses in the world to be inhabited by humans.

BEGINNINGS

The origin of New Zealand settlement is shrouded in mystery. The Maori, New Zealand's indigenous population, relied exclusively on oral tradition passed down through the centuries to tell their history and had no written language prior to European arrival.

According to legend, the Maori are believed to originate from east Polynesia. It is believed that Kupe, a chief of Hawaiki (the original home of Polynesian people), sailed to New Zealand about one thousand years ago. He is thought to have landed on Hokianga Harbor in Northland. He later returned to Hawaiki, calling the new land he'd found "Aotearoa," or "Land of the Long White Cloud." Kupe shared the sailing coordinates and encouraged others to go there. Over the next few centuries, more people did. When other Maori landed on New Zealand's shores, they brought with them the distinct Maori culture. The Maori on New Zealand were expert tattoo artists, carvers, and weavers.

The tale of Kupe's arrival in Aotearoa explains who discovered New Zealand but provides little detail. For instance, we do not know if Kupe sought the island out purposefully or if he happened upon it. In any case, the tale of Kupe's arrival is widely accepted, as it is one of the few

Abel Tasman was the first European to see New Zealand, in December 1642.

origin stories in existence. Historians believe there was either a massive migration to Aotearoa at some point or numerous voyages from Hawaiki delivered Polynesians to New Zealand over the course of hundreds of years. Whether frequent voyages, mass migration, or sporadic settlement initiatives led to the Maori population taking hold in New Zealand has never been firmly established. Nevertheless, it is believed that as many as 250,000 Maori may have been living in Aotearoa at the time of European arrival.

THE FIRST MAORI

The first Maori tribes in New Zealand survived by fishing and hunting the moa. Their diet was high in protein as a result of eating birds, fish, and shellfish. They also ate kumara, a sweet potato brought to New Zealand by early Maori settlers. The Maori were experienced horticulturists and grew several different varieties of kumara long before Europeans arrived.

The majority of the population lived on the northern coasts of North Island, where forests provided materials for shelter and clothing. Tribes moved across both islands and survived by growing food and through the trading of surplus food and treasured greenstone, or pounamu, as the Maori called it. Pounamu was often carved and used for ornamentation.

Tribal society was dependent upon blood ties and possession of land. Within the tribe, ancestry determined status. Those with demonstrable ties to tribal ancestors held leadership positions that affected the entire tribe. Land was communally owned and tribes were divided into semi-dependent groups, called *hapus*. Group settlements were situated around the *marae*, an open communal space. Violence sprung up between groups, often over limited food supply. When conflict occurred, the groups would move into fortified dwellings called *pas*, which were surrounded by intricate defensive earth structures.

EUROPEAN ARRIVAL

The Dutch navigator Abel Tasman was the first European to sight New Zealand, in December 1642. He called it "Staten Landt," but it was soon renamed "Nieuw Zealand," after a Dutch province. Tasman attempted to come ashore near what is now Takaka but lost four of his men when natives attacked the ship. Europeans would not return to settle the area for more than 150 years.

In 1769, Captain James Cook, an English explorer, was sent to the South Pacific on a scientific expedition. He circumnavigated the country and thoroughly surveyed its coastline. Unlike his predecessor, Cook was able to maintain a level of civility with the native inhabitants and made first landfall near the present-day city of Gisborne. Eventually, Captain Cook returned to England and shared what he had learned. His thorough definition of New Zealand's coastline encouraged whalers and traders to make their own voyages there. French and British sailors began to arrive, along with some Italians and Americans.

Seafaring expeditions seeking whale and seal blubber exploited the ocean's marine life, obliterating species in a matter of decades. Along with environmental destruction, Europeans brought foreign disease and firearms to the shores of New Zealand, which resulted in the death of scores of Maori people.

Captain James Cook mapped New Zealand's coastline.

When Europeans arrived in New Zealand, the Maori called them "pakeha," meaning "foreigner." Now the term refers to the white population of New Zealand.

THE FIRST SETTLERS

Three Christian missionary families formed the first organized European settlement in the country. The Reverend Samuel Marsden arrived from England in 1814 and preached his first sermon in the Bay of Islands on Christmas Day that year. By 1838, Bishop Jean-Baptiste Pompallier had founded a Roman Catholic mission in the same area.

The Treaty of Waitangi was signed on February 6, 1840. It was an agreement between the British crown and Maori chiefs. There were two versions, one written in English and one in Maori. Today it remains New Zealand's founding document.

Because the English and Maori versions of the Treaty of Waitangi carried different meanings on some points, by the 1860s the Maori people began to complain that they had been unfairly treated, particularly concerning the sale of their lands. Over the years, recognition of the treaty declined to a point where it was almost meaningless, having no legal status in domestic law. It was not until 1975 that the New Zealand Parliament set up the Waitangi Tribunal to investigate Maori claims against the British Crown from that year on. The law establishing the tribunal was amended in 1985 to permit the tribunal to examine claims dating back to the first signing of the treaty, on February 6, 1840. Many of these claims have now been made, and today the treaty has a unique place in New Zealand history—a partnership between cultures.

The vision of the early missionaries was one of a Christian and Maori New Zealand. However, commercial interests dominated subsequent developments. In 1839, Edward Gibbon Wakefield formed the New Zealand Company. It was directed by influential men in London commerce, who were eager to get the New Zealand economy going. They dispatched settlers to Aotearoa and profited by selling their newly acquired land to them.

By the 1840s there were about two thousand Europeans living in small settlements in New Zealand. Scattered throughout the country was a large transient population of whalers and traders. The Maori population, divided into independent tribes, traded extensively with the Europeans.

There was, however, no national government and no single set of formal laws. Maori land was being sold in a disorganized way. Some British settlers feared that New Zealand might be taken over by France, so Maori and pakeha, or European, groups asked Britain to provide some sort of protection and law and order.

This painting illustrates a European settler's hut in the Wairau Valley of New Zealand.

SETTLEMENT DISPUTES

Great Britain attempted to honor the Maori chiefs' request to recognize their independence, while at the same time extending British rule over New Zealand. It was hoped that British resident James Busby would bring about law and order in the country. Unfortunately, he lacked the means to enforce his authority and, as more and more immigrants arrived in New Zealand, disagreements between Maori and pakeha began to threaten lives and trade. Busby was replaced by William Hobson, a naval captain, who was sent to New Zealand in January 1840 to negotiate with the Maori for the sovereignty of the country.

Britain decided to make New Zealand a colony in order to control the European settlers and protect the rights of the Maori people. Hobson, Busby, and the missionary Henry Williams conceived the idea of drawing up a treaty that would be acceptable to both the British Crown and the Maori chiefs. On February 6, 1840, at Waitangi in the Bay of Islands, a treaty was read in English and Maori to more than four hundred Maori. After much debate and on the advice of Williams, the Maori chiefs agreed to give Queen Victoria of England sovereignty over their land. They accepted her protection and the offer of the same rights and duties of citizenship as the people of England, while still retaining their lands, forests, fisheries, and other possessions. More than forty signatures or marks were appended to the Maori text of the treaty, mostly by chiefs around the Bay of Islands. The Maori version of the Treaty of Waitangi was eventually signed by more than five hundred chiefs.

At first the treaty was recognized and observed as a contract that was binding on both parties, and in 1852, Britain allowed New Zealand to be

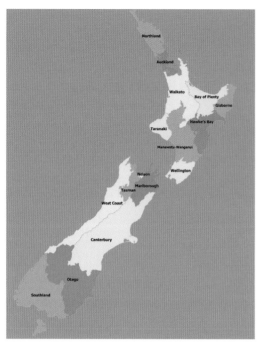

This map shows the sixteen local government regions New Zealand is comprised of.

self-governing. As people continued to migrate to New Zealand, there was increasing demand for land, and the Maori people became cautious about selling their land.

The law seemed to favor the pakeha. Conflict between settlers and the Maori finally led to land wars in the 1860s and the emergence of united tribes in the central North Island that had their own king. (The area is still known today as King Country.) Thousands of British troops were dispatched to control the Maori. During the land wars, the Maori won much admiration for their superb fighting and skill. During the Battle of Gate Pa (a *pa* is a fortified settlement), a Maori force of about 235 warriors defeated a combined British regiment and naval brigade of approximately 2,000 men who were much better armed than the Maori. However, the Maori eventually lost the war and their land due to the superior firepower of the British troops and the ever-continuing arrival of European settlers. It was at this point that New Zealand became a British colony in reality, not just on paper.

ECONOMIC GROWTH

Peace was not restored until 1870. Meanwhile, the discovery of gold in 1861 at Gabriel's Gully, Otago, a province in the South Island, marked the beginning of a major gold rush in New Zealand. The areas around Queenstown, Arrowtown, and Otago experienced a booming period of growth. In 1865, the capital was moved from Auckland to Wellington, and the Maori received representation in Parliament in 1867. New Zealand's first university, the University of Otago, was established in 1869 in Dunedin. The gold rush was over by the 1870s, but by then, agricultural industries had developed that could employ the growing population. The invention of refrigeration in the late 1800s meant that meat and dairy products could travel as far as England. Railways and roads were built so that produce could be transported to the coast and shipped all over the world. The government provided free public education. New Zealand was the first country to legalize unions in 1878 and also the first to recognize women's right to vote in 1893.

WARTIME

While New Zealanders were accustomed to domestic land disputes, the population was involved in its first international conflict when it supported Britain in the Boer War, fought in South Africa beginning in 1899. Over the course of the two-and-a-half-year conflict, 6,500 New Zealand soldiers and 8,000 horses, as well as teams of doctors, nurses, teachers, and veterinarians, sailed overseas to war. Of the soldiers, 71 died as a result of battle, while nearly 160 more died from diseases or accidents. This war would set the stage for the country's involvement in future world conflicts.

New Zealand soldiers fought for the British in World War I. Here, the soldiers inspect gas masks during the Second Battle of the Somme.

At the outbreak of World War I in 1914, New Zealand remained loyal to Britain by sending troops to Europe. New Zealanders were present at the battle at Gallipoli in Turkey, and 10 percent of the population joined the Australian and New Zealand Army Corps (ANZAC). New Zealand lost about eighteen thousand men from a population of only one million, largely due to a badly organized campaign by the British in Turkey. New Zealanders became disenchanted with the "motherland," and a sense of separate nationhood began to grow.

During World War II, New Zealand joined the Allied cause independently, officially declaring war on Germany on September 3, 1939. Over the course of the conflict, the country sent 140,000 men and women across the globe to various fronts, including Egypt, Italy, Japan, and the Pacific.

NATIONAL IDENTITY AND SOCIAL REFORMS

By the interwar period, many New Zealanders were proud of what they saw as their country's unique achievements in race relations. This, in turn, was one of the foundations for a belief that New Zealand had a special national role in the Pacific, and in the administration of other Polynesian peoples.

There were several outstanding men of Maori and mixed Maori ancestry who were leading members of Parliament and prominent intellectuals. Sir Apirana Turupa Ngata was a prominent New Zealand politician and lawyer who was also known for his work in protecting Maori language and culture. His portrait is on the New Zealand fifty-dollar note. Te Rangi Hiroa (Peter Buck) was a doctor who worked successfully with another Maori lawyer, Sir Maui Wiremu Pita Naera Pomare, to improve health and living conditions. Both men were members of Parliament.

From 1900 until 1965, New Zealand administered the Cook Islands, Niue, Tokelau, and Western Samoa (taking the last from the Germans during World War I). Although Western Samoa became the first Pacific island country to gain independence in 1962, the Cook Islands and Niue remain states in "free association" with New Zealand, and the Tokelauans voted to remain a New Zealand colony in 2007.

A period of industrial progress came during the 1920s, but the worldwide Great Depression (from 1929 until about 1939) hit New Zealand severely. The Labour Party, which had been formed out of various labor and trade unions and radical movements, won an election and formed its first government in 1935 under Michael Joseph Savage, leader of the Parliamentary Labour Party and prime minister of New Zealand.

A number of social reforms followed, including a social security system, a national health service, and a low-rent state housing program. The National Party also emerged during this period to represent more conservative and rural interests. It won the general election in 1949. The Labour and National Parties continue to compete in elections to form the government. Between 1935 and 2017, the Labour Party has controlled the government six times, while the National Party has controlled the government five times, sometimes in coalition with minor parties.

3

WITH A HISTORY THAT CAN BE complex at times, New Zealand's government has evolved as a partnership between cultures. Between Maori and pakeha, Kiwi and the Crown, the current New Zealand government is the result of years of compromise.

GOVERNMENTAL STRUCTURE

New Zealand is an independent state with a democratic form of government. While the government bears some similarities to other advanced nations, the New Zealand structure of government is unique. Much like the United States, New Zealand has three branches of government: the executive branch, the judicial branch, and the legislative branch. Each branch operates independently in an effort to ensure separation of power. Additionally, there are two other levels of government. They consist of regional councils and territorial authorities. Regional councils act like state governments in the United States, whereas territorial authorities act like city or county governments in the United States, but with more limited power. The central government—called the House of Representatives or, more commonly, Parliament—holds democratic elections every three years, while judges in New Zealand are not elected but appointed. There are four levels of courts and several specialized courts for specific legal matters.

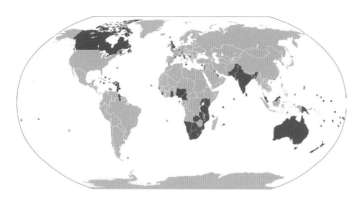

This map illustrates the countries that currently belong to the British Commonwealth.

ALL HAIL THE QUEEN

As a member of the British Commonwealth, New Zealand is formally headed by Queen Elizabeth II of Britain. The queen is represented in New Zealand by the governor-general, who is appointed by the queen, on the advice of the New Zealand government, for an unspecified term—generally three to five years. Early governors-general were often nobles from England. More recently they have been distinguished New Zealanders. Currently, Dame Patsy Reddy serves as governor-general, recommended by former prime minister John Key.

As the queen's representative, the governor-general opens Parliament, formally appoints the prime minister and other ministers, and signs legislation passed by Parliament. The governor-general has no discretion in such matters. He or she accepts the advice of the prime minister and the government that is in power. Only where there is no clear control of Parliament—and thus, no clear government—would the governor-general have more than a nominal role to play.

In recent years there has been some discussion about whether New Zealand should become a republic, replacing the sovereign with a government-appointed head of state. This would effectively raise the governor-general to the status of president, rather than a representative of the queen. Talk of the country becoming a republic has been more frequent in the twenty-first century, especially in the lead up to the 2017 election and following the nomination of Jacinda Ardern to prime minister. Ardern said she would welcome national debate on removing the queen as head of state.

SIMPLE STRUCTURE

New Zealand has perhaps one of the simplest structures of government of any advanced nation. It is composed of a central government, territorial authorities, and regional councils.

Like Britain, New Zealand is a parliamentary sovereignty. In other words, the will of Parliament rules supreme. The laws that Parliament makes are the rule of law for the country, and the role of the courts is to interpret them as they are written, without a formal document to guide them, other than the law itself, in decision making. Therefore, New Zealand does not have a single written constitution, like most other countries, but rather gets its sets of laws from various acts and agreements in its history.

Prime Minister Jacinda Ardern is seen here at a Parliament meeting in October 2017.

CONSOLIDATED POWER

The party or coalition of parties that controls Parliament decides who will be appointed as prime minister and other ministers. Each minister is given an area or areas of responsibility. The departments, which are part of the executive branch of government, that cover each area report to and are responsible to the minister in charge of that area. In other words, the group that controls Parliament also controls the executive. The judiciary is independent, but it cannot overturn laws passed by Parliament. Thus it is also subject to the laws passed by the group that controls Parliament.

Parliament once had two houses, but the second chamber was abolished in 1950. The single chamber that was retained consists of elected members of Parliament. Control of this body, which is won in elections held every three years, gives the winners control of Parliament.

Because of the range of responsibilities delegated to the central government, local New Zealand government is often overshadowed. Unlike in many countries, local authorities have no direct role in the provision of education or health services—these are the responsibility of the central government. As of 2017, there were seventy-eight local authorities within the country.

Elected local and regional government bodies are responsible for sewage, water supply, flood control, local roads, planning controls (for example, changes in land use and building permits), and provision of optional local leisure facilities, such as a sports stadium.

Thanks to the efforts of Kate Sheppard, on September 19, 1893, New Zealand became the first country in the world to grant women the right to vote.

ELECTIONS

Until the October 1996 general election, members were elected to Parliament by direct election from constituencies around the country. This usually meant that one party would win control of Parliament.

In this winner-take-all system, known in New Zealand as a first-past-the-post electoral system, votes cast for losing candidates were not reflected in the makeup of Parliament. Unhappiness with this system eventually resulted in a call for change from a first-past-the-post electoral system to one of proportional representation (an electoral system that aims at a close match between the percentage of votes that a group of candidates obtains in an election and the percentage of seats the group receives).

In two referenda held in 1992 and 1993, New Zealanders voted to adopt a system of proportional representation for Parliament called "mixed-member proportional" (MMP).

Under the old system, minor parties could gain a significant minority of votes, but still could not win any individual seats in Parliament. Under MMP, the number of seats that a party gains in Parliament is dictated by the proportion of the vote it receives nationally.

The first MMP election, held in October 1996, left a third party, New Zealand First, holding the balance of power between the Labour and National Parties. After lengthy negotiations, New Zealand First entered a formal coalition with the National Party in December 1996. Jim Bolger, the leader of the National Party, remained prime minister.

After the 2017 elections, a coalition government was formed between Prime Minister Ardern's Labour Party and Deputy Prime Minister Winston Peters's New Zealand First Party, with additional support from the Green Party.

LAWMAKING

Parliament is responsible for making laws, voting to "supply" funding to the government, and appointing the ministerial heads of the executive.

Proposed laws are placed before Parliament in the form of bills. These are debated both on the floor of the house and generally by a subcommittee of members of Parliament (MPs). A successful bill has to pass through three "readings," or votes, in Parliament before being sent to the governor-general for signature and passage into law. Most bills are introduced by the government of the day, although the opposition or individual MPs may also seek to introduce bills.

EXECUTIVE MATTERS

Executive governmental functions are carried out under the control of the ministers appointed by the governor-general. In practice, these ministers are chosen by the party or parties that control Parliament.

The Beehive, a slang term for the building that hosts New Zealand's executive branch, is located in Wellington City.

There are many staff employed by public service departments. The public service was substantially reorganized as part of widespread economic reforms in the 1980s. These reforms have greatly increased flexibility and accountability and sharpened efficiency. Under the State Sector Act of 1988, the chief executive of each public department is now accountable for running his or her department efficiently and effectively, and agrees on a contract of performance with the minister in charge of that department.

In this contractual relationship between ministers and department chief executives, the ministers decide what results they want and how much money is available. As in private sector firms, chief executives determine how they will accomplish the job. They have a large degree of freedom in this role.

Financial reforms in the Public Finance Act and elsewhere have required public departments to provide a high standard of financial disclosure, for instance, in distinguishing current expenditure from capital (investment) expenditure.

In public sector reforms and accountability, New Zealand is recognized as a world leader. Its system has been studied extensively by overseas delegations and international bodies.

One of New Zealand's most famous politicians, Sir Apirana Turupa Ngata, dedicated his life to preserving Maori culture. Ngata was born in a small town north of Gisborne. His father was a tribal leader, thus Ngata was raised in a Maori environment. He grew up speaking the language and engaging in Maori traditions. Ngata excelled in academics and was the first Maori to obtain a degree from a New Zealand university in 1893. He went on to become the first Kiwi to obtain a double degree in 1896 from the University of Auckland.

Elected to Parliament in 1905, Ngata quickly distinguished himself as an excellent speaker. He worked with other politicians to create legislation that encouraged more transparency in the sale and distribution of Maori land. During the First and Second World Wars, Ngata recruited Maori to fight for New Zealand. He served as minister of native affairs and even served as acting deputy prime minister occasionally.

Ngata is most well known for his dedication to Maori culture. He published a number of books on the subject, including a collection of traditional Maori songs. Ngata promoted and supported Maori sport through intertribal competitions. He also fought to preserve Maori dance and advocated for the Maori language to be taught at the University of New Zealand. Ngata was knighted in 1927 and died in 1950. Throughout his life, he worked to bring dignity to the Maori and pakeha alike. He is revered in the island nation, and a variety of educational institutions bear his name.

APPLYING THE LAW

Judges interpret and apply the law, and the judiciary is independent of the government. Aside from the main judicial system that includes district courts, the High Court, the Court of Appeal, and the Supreme Court, there are various specialist tribunals and courts in New Zealand. Most notable are the Employment Court (which considers employment disputes) and the Waitangi Tribunal (which considers claims arising under the Treaty of Waitangi).

The most senior court within New Zealand used to be the Court of Appeal. Appeals from lower courts could be made to this body, while appeals from the Court of Appeal could be made to the Judicial Committee of the Privy Council in England. However, the Privy Council, in reaching its verdicts, was bound by New Zealand statute. In 2004, the Supreme Court, based in New Zealand itself, replaced the Judicial Committee of the Privy Council in London as New Zealand's highest court of appeal.

CONFIDENTIAL ADVICE

The word "privy" means "private" or "secret." Thus, the Privy Council was originally a committee of the British monarch's closest advisors, who provided confidential advice on affairs of state. The Privy Council heard appeals and judgments that were made before January 1, 2004. After that point, the Supreme Court of New Zealand became the highest court in the nation and replaced the need for the Privy Council.

This photograph shows what the inside of the Supreme Court of New Zealand looks like.

The main form of law in New Zealand is New Zealand statute law—the law passed by the New Zealand Parliament. Subject to this are three other forms of law: common law (case law based on general rules developed by the courts, not only in New Zealand, but also, where relevant, in England and in other Commonwealth countries), United Kingdom statutes, and subordinate legislation (New Zealand statute may delegate some lawmaking powers to the governor-general and to local government).

INTERNET LINKS

https://www.beehive.govt.nz
Read speeches, view photos of state ceremonies, and learn more about the New Zealand government at this official website.

http://www.localcouncils.govt.nz/lgip.nsf
Curious about local government in New Zealand? Then check out this site, read articles about local ordinances, and view a map of the country that outlines the boundaries of local councils.

ECONOMY

New Zealand's colorful currency includes $20, $50 and $100 notes.

TODAY, NEW ZEALAND HAS AN advanced economy that has struggled to become less dependent on agrarian resources and access to British markets. The modern New Zealand economy is moving toward a more industry-focused free market economy that can compete on a global scale.

THE ECONOMY GROWS

From the 1860s on, New Zealand offered a high standard of living to most European settlers, so that an ordinary working-class family could enjoy meat on the table every day and a horse for transportation when these would have been nothing more than dreams for people in Europe. New Zealand's position, relative to other advanced economies, slowly declined during the twentieth century. However, from the mid-1990s on, the New Zealand economy began to expand, and its GDP grew a little faster than the OECD (Organization for Economic Cooperation and Development) average.

In 2016, the World Bank reported New Zealand's GDP at $185 billion US, with an annual growth rate of 3.9 percent. New Zealand is responsible for 0.3 percent of the world economy and has the fifty-third largest economy in the world. The country's currency is called the New Zealand dollar (NZD). About 76 percent of the working-age population is employed, and the median income is about $46,500 NZD annually, or about $32,000 US.

percentage of GDP, New Zealand has consistently attracted the highest levels of such investment of any advanced economy, often some $2 billion per year (3—4 percent of GDP).

Investment brings the capital, managerial skills, and contacts of overseas firms to New Zealand and demonstrates confidence in the economy. Many overseas managers work in New Zealand. The New Zealand seller (often the government) gains the sale price. But the sale means a loss of control to foreign investors, who will also look for a return on their investment.

COMMERCE

As a small economy, New Zealand is highly dependent on trade. With a relatively small workforce of 2.6 million, it has to specialize in certain industries and import many items, as there is insufficient manpower to cover all sectors of the economy.

For much of its history, the New Zealand economy has been dominated by the primary sectors of agriculture, fishing, forestry, and mining. In 1913, New Zealand's three main exports were (in descending order of importance) wool, meat, and dairy products. In 1983, the same three industries dominated exports, though dairy products had overtaken wool and meat. However, from the 1970s on, exports have diversified and now include forestry products, fish, and fruit. The manufacturing sector also grew in importance as an exporter, and tourism became a significant earner of foreign currency.

In 2016, total merchandise exports (excluding trade in services, such as tourism) were worth $32.5 billion. Key exports were dairy, meat, wood, fish, wool, fruit, crude oil, and wine. Until the mid-1970s, the main export market for New Zealand was Britain. Since then, New Zealand has diversified. Four markets are now of significant importance to New Zealand: Australia, Japan, China, and the United States.

KEY INDUSTRIES

DAIRY New Zealand's dairy sector accounts for $7.8 billion of the GDP. It makes up 3 percent of global dairy exports. The combination of low

population density, good infrastructure, and grass that grows rapidly makes New Zealand a highly competitive producer of dairy products.

Up until 2001, the New Zealand Dairy Board marketed dairy products overseas. That year, the Dairy Industry Restructuring Act came into play. It reorganized the dairy industry, combining the two largest dairy cooperatives into Fonterra. Today, Fonterra and Dairy New Zealand, funded by dairy farmers, represent dairy interests in New Zealand and around the world. Its headquarters are in the city of Hamilton.

MEAT AND WOOL Over one-quarter of New Zealand's land area is used for sheep farming. There are about six sheep for every person, and most are dual-purpose meat and wool animals. Teams of sheepshearers travel throughout the country, shearing wool from sheep, sometimes two hundred per day. New Zealand's main markets for meat are North America and the European Union.

Here, cows wait to be milked at a dairy farm. Dairy farming supports New Zealand's economy domestically and contributes to the world economy through exportation.

TOURISM Tourism has grown rapidly in recent years, with New Zealand's isolation luring more travelers to visit, rather than deterring them. The industry employs 7.5 percent of New Zealand's workforce. Some 3.5 million people visited New Zealand in 2016, with most visitors coming from Australia and China. Visitors generated $2.8 billion in tax revenue, while international tourism expenditure rose to $11.8 billion (a 17 percent increase from 2015) and contributed 17.4 percent to New Zealand's total export goods and services.

Tourists in New Zealand take in views from a ferry traveling from North Island to South Island.

FORESTRY In terms of the world's wood production, New Zealand is a small contributor, accounting for about 1.1 percent of the world's industrial wood and 1.3 percent of trade in forest products. Forestry accounts for about 3 percent of New Zealand's GDP, and the industry employs about twenty thousand New Zealanders. Commercial exotic plantation forests cover about 7 percent of New Zealand's land area. The main commercial tree species, *Pinus radiata*, accounts for 90 percent of the plantation area and can be harvested on a twenty-seven-year cycle—the fastest of any major supplier. New Zealand accounts for one-third of the world's radiata pines. Douglas firs occupy about 6 percent of the plantation area, while the remaining 4 percent consists of eucalypts and a variety of other species.

INFRASTRUCTURE New Zealand's international competitiveness and the quality of life of its population depend partly on its infrastructure. With a low population density, expenditure on roads per person is high. New Zealand relies heavily on sea transportation for overseas trade, although some high-value goods, such as flowers and seafood, are air-freighted for freshness to sophisticated markets such as Japan.

With deregulation of the ports in 1990, New Zealand's ports changed from some of the least efficient in the world to some of the most efficient, with port costs typically falling by one-half to two-thirds within two years. With the opening up of domestic air services to competition in 1987, airport and in-flight facilities improved virtually overnight.

TELECOMMUNICATIONS   New Zealand has the least regulated telecommunications sector in the world. Its largest supplier, Spark, has invested heavily in new technology, and prices have fallen rapidly. Today, New Zealanders own about 5.8 million cell phones—more than the country's total population—and 3.9 million people—or 88 percent of the population—are connected to the internet.

Spark is one of the nation's major telecommunications suppliers.

INTERNET LINKS

http://www.heritage.org/index/country/newzealand
A detailed analysis and comparison of New Zealand's economy to the rest of the world's countries can be viewed at the Heritage Foundation's 2017 Index of Economic Freedom website.

http://www.treasury.govt.nz/economy
New Zealand's Treasury Department website offers an overview of the country's economy as well as a breakdown of factors affecting prosperity and government initiatives targeted at growing the economy.

ENVIRONMENT

The natural environment is one of New Zealand's most precious resources.

5

NEW ZEALAND IS A NATION THAT HAS built its identity and wealth on the sanctity of its environment, so the Maori proverb to the right still resonates with the country's values. Kiwis enjoy a smorgasbord of geological forms, unique flora and fauna, and landscapes unlike any other place in the world. No matter where you are within the borders of the island nation, you are never more than about 80 miles (129 km) from the Pacific Ocean. While the country's landmasses are fairly narrow, they contain myriad features, including the mighty Southern Alps, towering glaciers, picturesque fjords, and even active volcanoes.

"Te toto o te tangata, he kai; te oranga o te tangata, he whenua." ("While food provides the blood in our veins, our health is drawn from the land.")
—Maori proverb

New Zealand's isolated location has allowed a number of endemic species to evolve, resulting in a one-of-a-kind biodiversity. Though the pristine environment attracts nature lovers worldwide, it is not without its disasters. Earthquakes and volcanic eruptions are characteristic of New Zealand and have been for thousands of years. Soil erosion and deforestation are long-standing issues. Thousands of species of

NEW ZEALANDERS

New Zealanders love to learn about and share culture.
Here, women learn Polynesian song and tradition at a
music festival.

6

WHILE THE QUINTESSENTIAL American humorist Mark Twain may have been making a joke at Kiwi expense when he made the statement, "If it would not look too much like showing off, I would tell the reader where New Zealand is," his comment illuminates the source of the independent and rugged spirit that characterizes New Zealanders.

Kiwis are a diverse group of people with a drive for innovation and invention birthed in part from an incredibly remote locale. Being removed from much of the world has meant that New Zealanders have literally had to fend for themselves. A citizenry made up of a variety of immigrants, Kiwis have had to figure out how to coexist despite differing perspectives. The pioneering spirit that led the first Polynesians to explore the shores also brought Europeans to the island nation. This shared drive to discover continues to define New Zealanders. Whether focused on preserving native arts or developing new adventure sports, Kiwis are motivated by their distant location and inspired by their legacy of innovation.

A GROWING NATION

During the first fifty years of European settlement (between 1831 and 1881), the European population of New Zealand increased from fewer than one thousand people to half a million. In 1886, 40 percent of these

Europeans were British. They came from England, Scotland, Wales, and Ireland. They came mostly from working-class and lower-middle-class backgrounds. It was the intention of the New Zealand Company and the government to populate New Zealand with Britons—to create a "Britain of the South." Today, New Zealand is a kaleidoscope of different peoples from Asia, Polynesia, and many other parts of the world.

These protestors are standing up for migrant and refugee rights in New Zealand in October 2017.

HONORS SYSTEM

New Zealand was oversold in Britain as a "Land of Promise" with very fertile soil, banana plantations, and other tropical fruit orchards. Steep hillsides covered in bush and scrub were described as "perfect for grapevines, wheat, and olives." A few aristocrats also moved to New Zealand, hoping to establish themselves as the elite of the new society. Many returned to Europe, finding life in New Zealand too tough. Nonetheless, the trappings of success from Europe soon arrived in New Zealand—large houses, servants, balls, fine clothes, and etiquette.

It was not long before the British government conferred honors on residents of the colony, such as "knights" and the female equivalent, "dames." Today New Zealand has its own honors system—a reflection of the confidence that New Zealanders have as a nation that stands apart from Britain.

A HISTORY OF MIGRANTS

Migrants came also from Australia (mainly whalers and sealers, but also escaped convicts), France, Germany, Scandinavia, Dalmatia, Lebanon, southern Europe, and Asia. As with the Australians, some of the American whalers and sealers also decided to make New Zealand their base. The Chinese came out to work in the gold fields of Central Otago in the 1860s and

INNOVATIVE TRANSPORTATION

As a result of New Zealand's remoteness and rugged landscape, its inhabitants have long been industrious and self-reliant. This hardy independence birthed a spirit of inventiveness, and Kiwis have been coming up with new tools, games, and gadgets for centuries. From specialized eggbeaters to extreme sports, a number of inventions have originated on the shores of the island nation. Many of the original designs that have come out of New Zealand are related to transportation.

As a child in Auckland, William Hamilton fantasized about navigating up the rivers of his home country. In 1954, Hamilton made his dream come true with the development of his jet boat, a propeller-free boat that could travel upstream. He continued to work with water-propulsion technology and founded one of the most successful water jet–manufacturing companies in the world.

The rough waters of New Zealand also inspired Alan Gibbs, a New Zealand businessman. Gibbs sought a way to traverse the tidal Kaipara Harbor and began experimenting with designs for amphibious vehicles in the 1990s. In 2003, he unveiled the Aquada (pictured above), the first street-legal high-speed amphibian. The Aquada can travel over 100 miles per hour (160 kilometers per hour) on land and over 30 miles per hour (48 kmh) on water. In 2004, fellow businessman Richard Branson drove an Aquada across the English Channel and set a new record for fastest crossing by an amphibious vehicle, at one hour and forty minutes—more than four hours faster than the previous record.

Other New Zealand inventions include commercial bungee jumping, the electric fence, the disposable hypodermic syringe, and the hand vacuum pump.

1870s (as did many Australians), and a large influx of Dutch migrants poured into the country after World War II.

Nestling on the slopes of pristine pastureland by the calm waters of Banks Peninsula (near Christchurch) is the historic French settlement of Akaroa. French street names and stone buildings with shutters preserve its Gallic heritage. The main street, Rue Lavaud, commemorates French seaman

Maori traditions such as dance and crafts are now a treasured part of the nation's cultural offerings.

Charles Lavaud, who captained the warship *L'Aube* that escorted Captain Jean Langlois's party of sixty-three immigrants from Rochefort in 1840. The Treaty of Waitangi and consequent British sovereignty over New Zealand ended Langlois's dreams of a French colony, but his settlers stayed on.

BRITAIN

Most New Zealanders are descendants of the early European settlers, mainly from Britain. Until fairly recently, Britain was considered the motherland of most New Zealanders, with thousands of people making pilgrimages home to the "old country" every year. Today, large numbers of people still visit Britain and Europe, but their purpose is more to experience life in another country than to rediscover their ancestral roots.

STARTING OUT

Unlike early North American settlements, most New Zealand settlers did not come to New Zealand for political or religious reasons. Instead, they came with the common goal of getting ahead in life, owning and establishing their own farms and small businesses. This common purpose was, to some extent, reflected in the motto of the first New Zealand coat of arms (an official symbol of New Zealand), which read "Onward." But the land was not as fertile as the earlier settlers had been led to believe, and a lot of hard work was needed to clear thick bush before farms could be established.

MODERN MAORI

As Anglo-Saxons became predominant in the community, Maori people, who had been dominant in 1840, became subordinate to the Europeans by 1890. Two societies then existed in New Zealand, although there was considerable

ADVENTUROUS SPIRITS

In adapting to their new environment, the early settlers had to make many compromises and improvisations. This has affected the way New Zealanders think of themselves today. "Kiwi ingenuity" is a common expression that epitomizes the positive attitude of New Zealanders when it comes to difficult or challenging situations, often involving the use of ordinary things to achieve extraordinary results. The stories of Richard Pearse and John Britten illustrate this New Zealand pioneering spirit.

RICHARD PEARSE *(1877–1953) was a Canterbury farmer who began the construction of his first aircraft in the late nineteenth century. He worked alone and without any financial backing. His aircraft had a bamboo and aluminum frame braced with wire. The aluminum came from flattened-out sheep-dip tins—large tins containing preparations of liquid disinfectant into which sheep are dipped to destroy parasites and to clean their wool, especially before shearing. Pearse's high-wing monoplane was mounted on bicycle wheels and had a span of about 26 feet (8 m). It was powered by a two-cylinder engine, which Pearse built himself.*

According to witnesses, he flew his aircraft for about 0.6 miles (1 km) on March 31, 1903, months before the famous Wright brothers made their first flight in America. Unlike the American brothers, however, Pearse did not go on to perfect his aircraft.

JOHN BRITTEN *In little more than a garden shed, John Britten (1950–1995), a Christchurch design engineer, toiled to design and build the fastest four-stroke motorcycle in the world, the Cardinal Britten V1000. A four-stroke is a kind of internal-combustion engine with a cycle of four strokes—intake, compression, combustion, and exhaust. This innovative bike has aerodynamics that are unequaled by other motorcycles and breathtaking sleekness. At its widest point, the Britten V1000's engine is no thicker than its rear tire.*

Britten's achievement was quite remarkable. European and American motorcycle magazine writers heaped praise on the Britten V1000 bike after it won the International Battle of the Twins (two-cylinder bikes) at Assen, Holland, in 1992.

For John Britten, designing bikes started out as a hobby. He also wanted to prove "that there is room for the individual to compete against the multimillion-dollar factory jobs." Now replicas of the Cardinal Brittens are being built for overseas collectors.

racial interaction between them, including some intermarriages between the Maori and Europeans. Separate schools for Maori and pakeha had the aim of preparing Maori for life among their own people and for Europeans to be trained in the professions, trade, and commerce. The Maori retained their traditional social structures and ceremonies, such as the hui (hoo-ee), a political and social gathering to which Europeans were often invited. Likewise, Europeans invited Maori chiefs to their balls and civic dinners.

By the early 1950s, the Maori population had recovered substantially in number, but they had lost control of a significant portion of their land during the land wars of the late nineteenth century. A shift from the rural areas to the towns and cities began, and by 1956 nearly a quarter of the Maori population were urban dwellers.

Various programs, including housing assistance, were established to help the Maori, especially the younger generation, adapt to urban living and integrate into mainstream pakeha society. In the rural areas, the Maori social structure follows the kinship networks of *whanau* (FAA-no-oo), or extended family; *hapu* (huh-POO), or subtribe; and *iwi* (ee-wee), or tribe. Within each tribe, there is a clearly defined system of rank and social control consisting of male and female elders, parents, uncles and aunts, religious mentors, and Maori wardens. When the Maori youth stepped out of these constraints— for instance, by moving to the cities from their tribal location—they found themselves in a completely different social structure. As a result, many fell into conflict with the law. Sadly, even today, there is a wildly disproportionate number of Maori offenders in New Zealand prisons relative to their share of the overall population of New Zealand.

A serious attempt was made through the support of voluntary associations (including churches and cultural and sports clubs) to help the Maori retain their cultural identity and spiritual values. Central to rural Maori life is the *marae* (mah-rye) with its ancestral house, where both religious and secular activities take place. Eventually, city *marae* were established. Today, there are even *marae* facilities on the campuses of secondary schools, colleges, and universities. However, for special occasions, such as weddings, Maori people journey back to their traditional tribal areas, to the *marae* where their ancestors debated important tribal decisions for generations.

TAKING ACTION

As they moved to the towns and cities, the Maori people learned much about the pakeha political and social systems that governed their lives, and they began to use radical and activist means to gain equality and social justice and a return of their assets, such as land and fisheries. Land became the symbol of Maori political subjection to pakeha laws and was a sensitive issue in the central government.

Though the controversial Treaty of Waitangi is centuries old, modern protests continue to highlight Maori struggles.

Today the Maori people represent 14 percent of the total population of New Zealand, and they are enjoying a cultural renaissance that continues to strengthen. They have their own television channel called Maori Television and many radio stations, which meet the needs of their communities. Access to such sources also helps preserve the Maori language and culture. However, there is still improvement needed in the treatment of the Maori in society and government as a whole.

On a political level, today the Maori have a bigger representation than previously in Parliament. Likewise, the Maori Council promotes the social and economic well-being of the Maori people and Maori culture. The council has won several court cases concerning land claims against the New Zealand government.

MODERN MIGRANTS

The fourth-largest ethnic group in New Zealand is the Pacific Island Polynesians, or Pacific peoples, whose members make up 7.6 percent of the total population. Today Auckland is the largest Polynesian city in the world, and small island territories such as Niue and Tokelau have more of their people in New Zealand than they do at home.

The Pacific Islanders have been flowing into New Zealand since the early 1960s, mainly for economic reasons. Young people from Pacific islands such as Western Samoa, Tonga, the Cook Islands, Niue, and Fiji have a greater potential for receiving a better education and finding employment in New Zealand than in their country of origin. A Ministry for Pacific Peoples ensures that the specific needs of the Pacific Islanders are met—for instance, for skills training and employment placement service—while at the same time recognizing the cultural values and aspirations of the Islanders.

Rugby is a sport celebrated professionally and recreationally in New Zealand. Here, two friends play touch rugby.

ASIAN MIGRANTS

Since the 1980s, an increasing number of Asian migrants have been coming to New Zealand. These include people from Taiwan, South Korea, Hong Kong, and mainland China. The Indian population is the fastest growing of the Asian populations in the country, and a corner "dairy" run by an Indian family is an institution.

The increasingly multicultural character of New Zealand has meant that Kiwi society has grown increasingly cosmopolitan and vibrant. No longer restricted to Maori and pakeha, each ethnic group contributes its own customs, culture, and influences to the New Zealand lifestyle.

REFUGEES

New Zealand has one of the world's highest intakes of refugees per head of population. Refugees from Europe arrived in the 1930s and again after World War II. Many of these were Jews and Poles. Following the 1956 Hungarian uprising, there was an influx of refugees from Hungary. In all, the country has resettled more than thirty-three thousand refugees since World War II. Today, New Zealand has a yearly quota of 750 refugees, though in 2015 it announced that it would take in an additional 600 refugees beyond that quota from war-torn Syria, spread out over three years. Each year, the country also allows 300 family members of resettled refugees to join their relatives in New Zealand.

The Communist victory and takeover of South Vietnam also resulted in an exodus of refugees. Since 1975, thousands of Indochinese refugees have been resettled in New Zealand. Other refugees include Chileans, Russian Jews, Eastern Europeans, and Assyrians.

POPULATION CONCERNS

Compared with most developed Western countries, New Zealand has always had a young population because of the large-scale immigration of mainly young adults and a high birth rate during the twentieth century. In 2017, the population growth rate was 0.79 percent.

INTERNET LINKS

https://youtu.be/w-uOHfbErE8
Watch the amazing Aquada, New Zealander Alan Gibbs's invention, traverse land and sea in this video.

https://www.youtube.com/watch?v=RryL3XwUO50
Watch this video to see a Hamilton water jet in action.

LIFESTYLE

New Zealand is known for being laid back. Here, teenagers in Queenstown relax with some ducks.

7

WHETHER ON THE NORTH, SOUTH, or any island within New Zealand, New Zealanders' infectiously upbeat attitude is present. This attitude isn't just present everywhere within the island nation; it also echoes throughout the daily lives of Kiwis. From school to work to special occasions, rural or urban life, New Zealanders spend less time worrying and more time being happy.

HOME LIFE

Family life in New Zealand is changing. Today, more people are waiting longer to get married. In 2015, the average age a man was likely to get married at was thirty, and twenty-nine was the average age of a woman marrying. There are many different kinds of families living in New Zealand as well. Although the traditional nuclear family still predominates, there are now de facto couple families, single-parent families, and same-sex couple families. The divorce rate is decreasing as well, perhaps related to more people waiting longer to marry.

THE STANDING PLACE

The Maori believe that a *marae* is their "standing place," somewhere, as a family, they know they belong. It is, in a sense, their "home." The

RELIGION

This church is known affectionately as the Cardboard Cathedral. It was built almost entirely of cardboard.

The form of Christian church services ranges from the very traditional (found in some Roman Catholic and Anglican churches), with full choirs and organ accompaniment, chants, formal prayers, and ritualistic observances, to a freer, more informal kind (seen in the evangelical and Pentecostal churches), with contemporary music and spontaneous singing by the congregation.

CHANGING FAITH

Today, many Kiwis are turning from an organized religious belief to either a more spiritual or secular belief system. According to a NewsHub article in 2016, more teenagers and migrants are remaining religious, while later in life, Kiwis and others are seeking different ways to express their religious beliefs, such as spiritualism rather than through organized religion. Some are abandoning religion altogether, as census statistics report.

INTERNET LINKS

http://www.globalreligiousfutures.org/countries/new-zealand#/?affiliations_religion_id=0&affiliations_year=2010&region_name=All%20Countries&restrictions_year=2015
Visit the Pew-Templeton Global Religious Futures Project web page to learn about how New Zealand's religious affiliation is expected to change in the coming years and how New Zealand compares to other countries.

https://www.teara.govt.nz/en/religion
The Encyclopedia of New Zealand's "Religion" page has a wealth of information about traditional Maori beliefs, differing sects of Christianity, and New Zealand's atheist community.

LANGUAGE

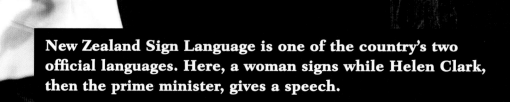

New Zealand Sign Language is one of the country's two official languages. Here, a woman signs while Helen Clark, then the prime minister, gives a speech.

9

I N NEW ZEALAND, ENGLISH IS BY FAR the most common language, with about 90 percent of the population being fluent, according to the 2013 census. As in the United States, however, despite the language's widespread use, English is not formally recognized by law as an official language of the country. Rather, the country has two state-recognized official languages: Maori and New Zealand Sign Language.

The Maori language, referred to as Te Reo, has been an officially recognized language since 1987, though just under 4 percent of the population reported speaking Maori in the 2013 census. While almost all Maori currently living in New Zealand speak English, only about one-quarter of them speak Maori. There is an effort being made to increase the number of speakers, and some schools offer Maori language classes. New Zealand Sign Language, the country's own language for the deaf, became an official language in 2006. It is not widely understood, with only 0.5 percent of the 2013 census population reporting fluency.

New Zealand has many popular sayings. Kiwis have an exuberance with language that both foreigners and natives find fun and refreshing.

GRAMMAR

People in New Zealand are educated in Standard British English. In fact, New Zealand English is more like British English than any other

"Ko te reo te tahuhu o tenei whare." ("Language is the ridgepole of this house.") —Maori proverb

Deaf New Zealanders and their loved ones use New Zealand Sign Language (NZSL) to communicate. While it is similar to American and British Sign Language, there are some key differences. In 2000, the lexical differences between the three languages were compared, and it was discovered that NZSL and British sign Language are about 63 percent similar, while NZSL shares only about 33 percent of signs with American Sign Language. NZSL is more reliant on lip movement than British Sign Language and also has unique vocabulary to describe certain Maori concepts and New Zealand landmarks.

Though it is now an official language, the evolution of NZSL was not without controversy. The first known teacher of sign language in New Zealand was Dorcas Mitchell, who taught dozens of deaf pupils in Lyttelton Harbour in 1877. The following year, New Zealand's first school for the deaf opened, and Mitchell applied for the job of principal but was passed over. Gerrit van Asch, an educator who believed deaf people should learn exclusively through oral instruction, became principal instead. Sign language was forbidden at the school until 1979. Despite it being outlawed, students continued to use sign language covertly, and it developed this way for over one hundred years. In 1979, instructors began teaching Australian Sign Language and adopted NZSL for instruction in 1994. In 1998, a comprehensive NZSL dictionary containing about four thousand signs was published by Victoria University of Wellington and the Deaf Association of New Zealand. After a lengthy period of development, NZSL became an official language in April 2006.

non-European variety. The national newspapers and public documents are written in Standard English. Nevertheless, Maori words have found their way into the vocabulary, and the language has been influenced by both Australian and American English.

When they are overseas, New Zealanders are often mistaken for Australians, but to a New Zealand ear, the Australian accent sounds quite different—just as a Canadian accent is noticeable to an American. The main difference concerns the short "i" vowel. The Australian term *fish and chips* sounds like "feesh and cheeps" to a New Zealander, who would pronounce it "fush and chups," and *Sydney* sounds like "Seedney." However, the practice of turning a statement into what seems like a question—what phonetic experts call high-rising terminal intonation—is common to both.

INTONATION

New Zealand pronunciation departs from Standard British English in the intonation of vowel sounds, particularly in closing diphthongs (a diphthong is a syllable that

combines the sounds of two vowels). For example, *today* sounds like "todie," *high* sounds like "hoi," *hello* sounds like "helleouw," and *trout* sounds like "treout." Another common trait is the centralized "i," producing "ut" for *it* and "paintud" for *painted*. Since the early 1960s, the distinction of vowel sounds in words like *ear* and *air*, *here* and *hair*, and *beer* and *bare* have become less pronounced.

COLLOQUIALISMS

There are many compounded words, new meanings, and colloquial expressions in the language that derive from a specifically New Zealand experience and environment. Examples are *cow-cockie* (dairy farmer), *section* (plot of land), and *up the boohai* (a *boohai* is a remote district or area; *up the boohai* means "very much awry").

TE REO

New Zealand Maori is a Polynesian language closely related to Cook Islands Maori, Tahitian, and Hawaiian. It is the first language of some fifty thousand adult Maori New Zealanders (12 percent of the Maori population). One of the most important aspects of the Maori renaissance of the 1970s was the renewal of interest among the Maori in their indigenous language. There are more speakers of Maori now than there were at the beginning of the twentieth century.

Use of the Maori language was encouraged through a Maori-language preschool movement and by Maori-language immersion primary schools. The former is a *whanau*, or extended family base, where very young children are taught traditional knowledge, crafts, and customs through the medium of the Maori language. Maori-language immersion primary schools teach pupils the entire school curriculum in Maori. Thousands of secondary school pupils also take Maori language as a subject. In fact, there are a number of schools where students are taught in the Maori language at least 51 percent of the time. A Maori Language Commission assists government departments and other agencies in offering a range of services in Maori.

INTRODUCING READING AND WRITING

When the first missionaries arrived in New Zealand, the Maori did not have a written form of language. Their genealogies were recorded in stylized figures carved on the wooden poles of their ancestral meetinghouses, while folk art related their myths and legends. Then, in 1820, two Anglican missionaries traveled back to England, taking with them two important Maori chiefs. At Cambridge University in England, they produced the first Maori grammar.

This important work was further developed during the next decade by the missionaries. The Maori people were so eager to learn that they would use gunpowder instead of chalk when the latter was not available to them. By the mid-1830s, Maori who wished to be held in high regard recognized the need to be literate.

MAORI VOCABULARY

Language is always changing, and the Maori were quick to extend their vocabulary to take foreign ideas and objects into account. Maori people began to fit foreign words to their own phonology. For example, *Hune* (HOO-ne) means "June," *moni* (mor-nee) means "money," and *hipi* (hip-ee) means "sheep."

Today, Maori speakers like to adapt Maori words and phrases to express new ideas and objects. Maori vocabulary has also found its way into New Zealand English. Most of these borrowed words are nouns—for example, bird names such as *kiwi* and *kakapo*, plant names such as *manuka* and *kumara*, and trees such as *kauri* and *rimu*. Other Maori words add a richness of expression, such as *mana*—used to connote a person's prestige, status, or honor. *Mana* is a very important concept in Maoridom.

There are very many places in New Zealand with Maori names, including mountains, rivers, and lakes. Some of these have an English name as well.

For example, Mount Taranaki is also called Mount Egmont. In tourist centers such as Rotorua and Queenstown, public information signs are displayed in several languages.

This bilingual sign features a warning written in English and Maori.

Every syllable in Maori should be pronounced clearly and must end with a vowel. Practice sounding the syllables separately at first, then run them together. For example, say "Maa-or-ri" for *Maori*. There are five vowel sounds, each of which may be said either short or long. The vowels sound like the following:

short *a*, like *u* in *hut*

long *aa*, like *a* in *Chicago*

short *i*, like *i* in *hit*

long *ii*, like *ee* in *keep*

short *e*, like *e* in *fleck*

long *ee*, like *ai* in *fair*

short *o*, like *or* in *distort*

long *oo*, like *ore* in *sore*

short *u*, like *u* in *put*

long *uu*, like *oo* in *spoon*

Maori diphthongs retain the sound of the second vowel quite clearly, and most of them are not matched in sound by anything in English. For example, *ae* sounds like the "igh" in *high*.

Consonants are pronounced as they are in English, with the exception of *wh*, which sounds more like "f," and *ng*, which always sounds like the "ng" in the nasal-sounding *clanger* rather than *linger*.

INTERNET LINKS

http://www.tetaurawhiri.govt.nz/the-landscape-of-aotearoa-will-resonate-with-our-indigenous-language
The Maori Language Commission seeks to promote the everyday use of Maori as a living language. Visit their website here.

https://www.youtube.com/watch?v=CbDf0YG2xnA
Watch interpreters sign the New Zealand National Anthem in NZSL using both English and Maori signs.

ARTS

These dancers are performing a haka, a traditional Maori dance, in honor of Shakespeare's birthday.

10

FROM A TIME WHEN ONLY MAORI tribes roamed the land to New Zealand's modern multicultural society, art has played an important part in forming the country's national identity. With ancient roots in weaving, carving, and tattooing, the Maori art-making practices continue to be honored by current natives and foreign travelers.

European arrival ushered in an era of portraiture, during which many Maori people were painted or drawn by new arrivals. These portraits were shared with European citizens, and for the first time, people who had never set foot on New Zealand soil could visually observe Maori aesthetics and customs. Visual art continues to flourish in a variety of forms. From carvings to landscape paintings, New Zealand artists continue to be inspired by their history and surroundings.

New Zealand's literary history is also steeped in a diversity of influences. Poets, short-story writers, children's authors, and novelists have called the island nation home and helped to cultivate New Zealand's literary profile.

Kiwis also celebrate music and dance in their culture. From the modern performance of the ancient war dance haka (huh-kuh) to the revered opera houses, it is clear that performance and song are ingrained in the New Zealand people. One art form that supports New Zealand's native expression and draws foreign artists to its shores is filmmaking. Both tourists and natives have countless opportunities to participate in New Zealand's historical and modern interpretations of beauty.

"Kaore a te rakau whakaaro, kei te tohunga te whakaaro." ("The wood has no thoughts, such only belong to its carver.")
—Maori proverb

ALL LEISURE
BLACKS

New Zealand's professional rugby team, the All Blacks,
is by far the most beloved team in the country.

11

S PORT IS ONE OF NEW ZEALAND'S most valued pastimes. Sporting has played a huge role in shaping New Zealand's national image. Achieving against all odds, overcoming hurdles and difficulties, and facing a challenge head-on are all prized qualities, both on and off the playing field.

The late New Zealand mountaineer Sir Edmund Hillary, who, in 1953, became the first man in the world (with Sherpa Tenzing Norgay) to reach the top of Mount Everest, is a prime example of this conquering spirit. From Hillary's summit to the absolute dominance of the lauded national rugby team, the All Blacks, Kiwis have been taking part in friendly but fierce competition for decades. For those New Zealanders who prefer to unwind in a more relaxing way, there are a variety of outdoor activities to engage in amid some of the most beautiful landscapes in the world.

COMPETITION

Competitive sporting activities are not just favored as entertainment. They are part of the compulsory education system. The international caliber of New Zealand's athletes has contributed a great deal to the cultural identity of New Zealand. Government policy ensures that sports, fitness, and leisure activities are available to all who wish to participate, including people with disabilities. The Hillary Commission for Sport, Fitness, and Leisure worked from 1987 until 2003 to provide public funding for sporting and leisure activities in New Zealand. Today, the organization Sport New Zealand performs much the same function.

PROFESSIONAL SPORTS

Rugby is the national sport, with the internationally renowned All Blacks starring as a symbol of national identity. The first World Cup Rugby competition in 1987 was won by the All Blacks. The team also won the World Cup in 2011 and 2015. The All Blacks derive their name from the color of their uniform—a black jersey and pants.

Much effort has been made to try to keep politics out of the sporting arena. However, in 1981, an exclusively all-white Springbok team from South Africa toured New Zealand. This upset many New Zealanders and caused protests.

Cricket has been played in New Zealand for over 150 years and is New Zealand's oldest organized sport. There are both men's and women's cricket teams. New Zealand secured its first test win in 1956, beating the West Indies, and its first test series (a set of test matches played between two teams

Cricket is the nation's oldest organized sport.

MODERN LAND DIVING

The spirit of Kiwi innovation has touched all aspects of New Zealand culture, including extreme sport. AJ Hackett, a Kiwi entrepreneur, was inspired by a peculiar ancient practice and updated it, creating one of the most popular activities among adrenaline junkies: bungee jumping.

For centuries, the people of Vanuatu (an island nation in the South Pacific) have thrown themselves from huge wooden towers using only vines tied to their feet to stop them from falling to their deaths. They call the practice land diving, and it remains a cultural staple for the people of Vanuatu. In the 1970s, the Oxford University Dangerous Sports Club performed some experimental jumps modeled after Vanuatu land diving. Hackett was inspired by these videos in the 1980s, along with his friend Henry van Asch. They set about devising a modern alternative to the simple vines used by the people of Vanuatu and collaborated with scientists at Auckland University to develop the first bungee cords. Once a suitable cord was developed, Hackett knew he would need to make a publicized jump to garner attention for the burgeoning extreme sport.

In June 1987, he and van Asch snuck onto the Eiffel Tower under the cover of darkness. The next morning, Hackett jumped from the towering landmark. He was immediately arrested but was released shortly after. The stunt worked, and the world's first commercial bungee-jumping site opened at the Kawarau Bridge in November 1988. New Zealanders and foreigners alike couldn't wait to try bungee jumping and paid seventy-five dollars each for the thrill.

Bungee jumping introduced adventure tourism to New Zealand, and both visitors and natives enjoy the adrenaline rush of bungee jumping both at home and around the world.

representing different countries for a championship), against Pakistan, in 1969. Since then, New Zealand has had particular success in international one-day matches, which are very popular with television viewers. The introduction of one-day matches has resulted in greater participation in the sport; it is now New Zealand's fastest growing sport at the junior level. Sir Richard Hadlee was one of the sport's outstanding players. He retired in 1990 with the world record at the time for wickets taken in test matches—431. He

VACATION

Backpacking is a favorite pastime of both native New Zealanders and tourists.

Going on vacation is part of the Kiwi lifestyle. Usually vacations are taken in summer, mainly in January, though many people will take winter breaks to the ski fields. Families flock to camping grounds near the sea or the lakes, where they can fish, swim, water ski, canoe, or sail their yachts. Some of the faster-flowing rivers are ideal for white-water rafting, while others are great for jet boat rides. Many people stay in the family bach, or small cottage. The bach, often set in a fairly remote area and containing the barest essentials, offers relaxed and simple living.

The weekend retreat to the bach or a place in a rural area is popular with those who have demanding or very busy lives. It is a chance to explore the countryside, perhaps on horseback or in tough four-wheel-drive vehicles. The more adventurous enjoy hang gliding, parachute jumping, or deep-sea diving.

When they are not making the most of their clean, green environment, New Zealanders love to read. In fact, it is estimated that they read and buy more books per head of population than any other English-speaking country.

AROUND THE HOUSE

Family life centers around the home. Houses range in style from late nineteenth-century cottages to very modern, individually designed homes. Regional and climatic differences influenced the way the early settlers housed themselves. Large-windowed timber houses with their open verandas in Northland contrast with the stone buildings and their smaller windows in Southland, where the climate is much cooler.

Today, there is more emphasis on indoor/outdoor living styles, with wide glass doors that open directly onto balconies, patios, or gardens. Apart from the comparatively few inner-city apartment blocks, each house is detached, sitting on its own land. Many have two stories, while some have their own swimming pools and tennis courts. A shift away from small houses on large plots to large houses on smaller plots is noticeable. It is still the aim of the majority of New Zealanders to own their own home. However, home ownership rates have decreased after hitting a peak in 1991. This is attributed to a number of factors, the main one being the higher cost of home ownership. The average home costs $900,000 to $1,000,000 NZD (about $617,000 to $688,000 US) in cities such as Auckland and Manukau. This is a higher price than in many other developed nations, making it more difficult for people to own property. As a nation of "do-it-yourselfers," New Zealanders devote a lot of energy and leisure time to home improvements.

European-style houses dot a hillside on Mount Victoria in Wellington.

Gardening is a favorite hobby for thousands of New Zealanders. There are cottage gardens, wild gardens, formal gardens, herb gardens, native plant gardens, exotic gardens, and specialist gardens. Flower shows and television and radio programs keep keen gardeners up to date with the latest techniques and hybrids.

INTERNET LINKS

http://www.allblacks.com
Watch video and read articles about New Zealand All Blacks, the dominant national rugby team.

http://nzc.nz
Learn about New Zealand cricket and watch the Black Caps, New Zealand's professional cricket team, in action.

https://www.youtube.com/watch?v=T-4TzSPlqX4
Watch bungee-jumping enthusiasts fall from a variety of New Zealand locales.

FESTIVALS

The Queenstown Winter Festival hosts an event where participants launch themselves into the freezing waters of Lake Wakatipu.

12

"New Zealand is not a small country but a large village."
—Peter Jackson, movie director

THOUGH HALF A WORLD AWAY FOR most visitors, New Zealand offers a close-knit, laid-back yet enthusiastic cultural experience for travelers, which is on full display at the many festivals hosted in New Zealand throughout the year. From honoring military veterans to massive rock music festivals to Maori New Year ritual celebrations, gatherings in New Zealand can draw huge crowds, but festivalgoers often feel a strong sense of community.

NATIONAL HOLIDAYS

New Zealand's national holidays include New Year's Day, Waitangi Day, Easter, ANZAC Day, the Queen's Birthday, Labor Day, and Christmas. Waitangi Day and ANZAC Day are particularly significant, as they mark turning points in the nation's history.

But festival fun is not confined to national holidays. Throughout the year and around the country, the events calendar is crowded with a great many activities, such as country music festivals, hot-air balloon fiestas, film festivals, air pageants, opera festivals, music fests, fashion shows, spring blossom festivals, and art and craft shows.

New Zealand's wide cultural mix is celebrated in Chinese dragon boat races, Welsh choral singing festivals, Japanese festivals, Irish and

Of all the celebratory events enjoyed by New Zealanders, music festivals might be the most dynamic. With a calendar of several annual events that feature a variety of acts, the enthusiasm for live festival entertainment is immeasurable, but the most anticipated events occur around the New Year. Several festivals have emerged as favorites among Kiwi music lovers who are looking to ring in the new year.

Rhythm and Vines is a three-day celebration that is held in Gisborne from December 29 until December 31. Founded in 2003 by students at the University of Otago, Rhythm and Vines holds the distinction of being the first festival in the world to see the first sunrise of each new year. International superstars like N.E.R.D., Chromeo, Public Enemy, Franz Ferdinand, Wiz Khalifa, and Empire of the Sun have graced the stages of Rhythm and Vines. In fact, according to the festival's organizers, 11 percent of tickets are sold to international festivalgoers. In recent years, the festival has added comedy events and even featured motocross riders flying across the main stage in 2015.

Highlife is another New Year's music event popular in New Zealand. Years past have seen the event hosted as an NYE experience, but in 2018 the event was a New Year's Day celebration occurring on January 1. The event was held at Smales Farm in Auckland and featured local DJs, musicians, dancers, and a variety of other performers.

Northern Bass is also held in Auckland and highlights DJs, producers, hip-hop artists, and other performers. It runs from December 29 until January 1. Rhythm and Alps occurs simultaneously in Cardrona Valley, which is located in the Southern Alps. The festival is a highlight of the season for the South Island and sees about ten thousand attendees each year. It features four stages and aims to give festivalgoers an intense sound and light show.

No matter what kind of music you enjoy, if you find yourself in New Zealand during New Year's, there are plenty of entertainment options.

Scottish cultural festivals, and Asia-Pacific and Maori performing arts festivals. Queenstown's Winter Festival is a week of entertainment and revelry.

COMMEMORATING A TREATY

Every year on February 6, a celebration takes place to commemorate the signing of the Treaty of Waitangi in 1840. Maori tribal leaders and many others join the governor-general, the prime minister, and leading dignitaries in a formal ceremony on the grounds of the Treaty House at Waitangi.

ANZAC Day honors all New Zealand soldiers and pays tribute to the soldiers who fought in World War I during the Gallipoli campaign.

It is a time for New Zealanders, in particular the Maori and pakeha, to reflect on their past, to appreciate the progress that has been made toward the unification of the two peoples, and to consider the way to move in the future. Waitangi Day focuses attention on the implications of the founding document of the nation.

Over the years, the government has faced numerous claims by Maori tribes. Nevertheless, there is still more to be achieved. Indeed, Waitangi Day celebrations are traditionally peppered with Maori protesters.

A DAY TO CELEBRATE THE ARMY

ANZAC stands for "Australian and New Zealand Army Corps," a group that was formed during World War I. On April 25, 1915, at dawn, the ANZAC landed on the beach of Gallipoli in Turkey, which was defended by the Turks. They gallantly fought a campaign that had been planned by British politicians and was led by British officers. Thousands of lives were lost, and so was the campaign.

However, the courage of the ANZAC in what was an impossible situation led to a celebration of the landing after the war was over. The returned soldiers paraded through the streets of London to receive honor from the king and queen outside Buckingham Palace (the official London residence of the British monarch). It marked the beginning of a new "mateship" between the Australians and New Zealanders. Today, the word "ANZAC" is often used to describe a combination of effort between the two countries.

ANZAC Day, celebrated every year on April 25, is a time for New Zealanders to remember and honor their soldiers and heroes from all wars. The day starts with parades at dawn throughout the country. Old soldiers proudly wearing their medals march behind military and other brass bands to a central point of commemoration—usually a cenotaph (a monument built to honor soldiers

STARS MARK THE NEW YEAR

New Zealand hosts a unique series of festival events centered around the Maori celebration of the new year, known as Matariki. The word Matariki also refers to the cluster of stars known to astronomers as the Pleiades. The cluster's rising in midwinter holds great significance on the Maori lunar calendar (also known as Maramataka) as it signals the time for harvest along with the beginning of another year. The Maori have many legends regarding the cluster of stars known as Matariki. One of the more popular legends views the largest star as the "mother," while the surrounding stars are her six "daughters." Every year the mother and daughter stars are said to be traveling across the sky in preparation for a visit with their "great grandmother," Mother Earth. Each star has a distinct personality, which serves to remind the Maori people of what is important in the year to come. For example, the eldest daughter star is said to spend her time with her great grandmother cultivating plants so that they can grow strong and be productive. This reminds Maori people to foster their strengths along with the strengths of the community.

Traditionally, Matariki has been celebrated with a remembrance of ancestors, the lighting of ritual fires, Maori dancing, singing, and offerings made to celebrate life and honor the dead. Bidding farewell to the dead is a significant part of Matariki as loved ones who had died the previous year were believed to shine down from the heavens as stars.

who died in a war) on which the names of the fallen soldiers from the area are inscribed.

Many civilians, both young and old, join them. Traditionally, the ANZAC service includes a trumpet fanfare, "The Last Post." Wreaths are laid, hymns are sung, and speeches are made. A national service is held in Wellington, presided over by leading officials who represent the military, government, diplomats, and the church.

CHRISTMAS TRADITIONS

Christmas festivities in New Zealand begin around the middle of November with colorful street parades and brightly decorated shops. Although Christmas takes place in summertime in New Zealand, Santa Claus still arrives in a reindeer-driven sleigh, warmly dressed in his Nordic costume. Little children climb onto his knee in department stores and shopping malls to request toys and presents. Many of the traditions of the Northern Hemisphere are

The annual Farmers Santa Parade has brought joy to the residents of Auckland since 1933.

followed, including the preparation and baking of large Christmas fruitcakes and mince pies.

Gifts are exchanged on Christmas Day, which is traditionally the time when extended families get together to celebrate the festive season. Young children get up very early to see if Santa Claus has brought all the things they asked for, in exchange for the drink and piece of cake they left out for him the night before. Carols (both traditional and contemporary, reflecting Christmas in the Pacific) are sung in the churches and outdoors by candlelight.

GOOD FRIDAY AND EASTER

Good Friday and Easter Monday are public holidays in New Zealand. Many Christians give up a favorite food during Lent (a period of forty days from Ash Wednesday to Holy Saturday), which leads up to Easter, as this is a time when they remember the death of Jesus.

Special foods that are traditional at Easter include hot currant buns topped with white icing in the shape of a cross, which are symbolic of Jesus's death, and chocolate eggs, which are symbolic of new life and Jesus's resurrection. Easter is also a time for special events, such as fairs, craft shows, car rallies, and club activities.

OTHER SPECIAL DAYS

LABOR DAY This holiday was introduced in 1899 to commemorate the eight-hour workday. It falls on the fourth Monday of each October.

QUEEN'S BIRTHDAY A public holiday is celebrated on the first Monday in June to mark Queen Elizabeth II's birthday, which is actually in April. Usually the only "celebration" involves the firing of twenty-one cannon balls as a salute to the queen.

NEW YEAR'S DAY This holiday is really celebrated in style on New Year's Eve—leaving many people tired the next day after celebrating late into the night.

Each province also has its own anniversary day to mark its beginnings. From time to time, important events are reenacted in period costume, such as the landing of the early settlers on the beaches of the capital city.

NEW ZEALAND FESTIVAL

Every two years, the New Zealand Festival is staged in Wellington, centering on the arts. This three-week event attracts high-caliber international artists and visitors from around the globe. People can immerse themselves in every kind of artistic activity, from large-scale opera to mime and street art. In 2016, there were more than four hundred performances involving 1,200 artists from twenty-five different countries. Seven New Zealand works also premiered there. Over 110,000 people attended events throughout the festival period.

INTERNET LINKS

http://www.festival.co.nz
Learn about the New Zealand Festival, a biannual celebration that features a variety of live arts performances across New Zealand from mid-February to mid-March.

https://www.nziff.co.nz
Watch trailers, read reviews, and view schedules for films featured at New Zealand International Film Festival events.

https://www.tepapa.govt.nz/learn/matariki-maori-new-year/matariki-festival-2017
Watch highlights from the 2017 Matariki Festival events and learn all about Matariki rituals at this Museum of New Zealand website.

FOOD

Lolly cake is a delicious dessert unique to New Zealand.

13

"Kia ki ki te rourou iti a haere." ("Let the small basket of the wayfarer be filled.")
—Maori proverb, used when giving food to a traveler

LIKE THE REST OF NEW ZEALAND'S culture, its food is reflective of a variety of resources and cultural influences. European, Middle Eastern, and Pacific influences have blended to produce a unique culinary culture.

New and creative ways of food preparation and presentation have evolved from a blend of ethnic influences to produce what is described as Pacific Rim cuisine. New Zealand's seasonally available local ingredients drive culinary trends even as diverse cooking influences and methods flourish. Despite the integration of modern influences, traditional Maori food and cooking methods remain valued elements of Kiwi cuisine. Both food and drink are distinctive in New Zealand, as the nation has a thriving wine market and a history of brewing craft beer.

The wealth of produce available in New Zealand is astonishing. Local farms produce venison, lamb, olive crops, and even wasabi on a seasonal schedule. Cherries, garlic, and a variety of berries are also grown domestically. One of New Zealand's resources never out of season is the ocean. New Zealanders are spoiled with fresh offerings of seafood. From delicious salmon, snapper, and blue cod to crayfish and trout, the waters surrounding the island nation contain a smorgasbord of delicacies.

SEAFOOD

New Zealand's seafood availability is enough to make a food enthusiast's mouth water. One favorite is the lobster, or crayfish as they are called locally. There are two native species in New Zealand, the spiny red

Greenshell mussels are one of the nation's many seafood delicacies.

rock lobster and the packhorse crayfish. Both are found throughout New Zealand waters, but the red rock lobster is by far the most common. Kaikoura is a treasured crayfish spot in New Zealand. In fact, the name Kaikoura literally means "eat crayfish" in Maori. Tourists might be shocked at expensive prices on restaurant menus, but there are remedies for this. Trained divers are able to harvest their own catch in New Zealand waters. Visitors who don't dive are encouraged to stop at Kaikoura Seafood BBQ Kiosk in Kaikoura, a small beachside establishment that serves up delicious crayfish for a reasonable price.

Another one of New Zealand's signature seafood delicacies is the greenshell mussel. The greenshell mussel is unique to New Zealand and is so named because of its dark brown/greenish shell that has green tips. Most of the greenshell mussels wash ashore Ninety Mile Beach in northern New Zealand. About 20 percent of the aquaculture is farmed.

A mussel farm consists of a series of buoys held together by long lines attached to each side of the buoy. The line is anchored to the sea floor at each end. From the long lines, a series of weighted ropes hang down, but they do not reach the bottom. Young mussels attach themselves to the rope and are then left to grow. After fourteen to eighteen months, when the mussels have reached the desired size, the rope is lifted and the mussels are harvested. Greenshell mussels can be prepared in a variety of ways, but they are often served simply in a half-shell and can be flavored with anything from garlic butter to red pepper.

King salmon, also called chinook, is a popular New Zealand seafood dish. This particular species of salmon has the highest natural content of omega-3 oil, which is believed to support a healthy heart and joint function. New Zealand produces just over half of the world's supply of king salmon, with some of the freshest stock available within its borders. Many fine-dining establishments serve king salmon grilled, smoked, or as sashimi—raw and thinly sliced.

Whitebait, arguably New Zealand's favorite fish featured in its cuisine, is one of the country's more expensive delicacies. These tiny juvenile fish are caught in freshwater rivers and lakes and served fried in patties or cooked with eggs (called fritters). These tiny fish are very hard to catch, and they can only be fished from mid-August until late November. Competition for fishing locations and the challenge that catching whitebait poses drives up menu costs. The rivers on the South Island's west coast often offer the largest volume of whitebait to fishers.

Oysters enjoy a wonderful reputation in New Zealand, but none is more sought after than the Bluff oyster. This oyster is endemic to New Zealand and grows in Foveaux Strait just off the coast of Bluff, the country's southernmost town. The prized oysters are said to be briny and sweet with a tangy metallic finish. These delicacies are rare as only about ten million are pulled from the waters every year. These local favorites are so well loved that each May, the Bluff Oyster and Food Festival attracts thousands of visitors to the modest southern town.

MAORI INFLUENCE

When Maori arrived in what is now New Zealand, they had to adapt to the offerings of the land when determining how they would feed themselves. Hunters and gatherers who depended on both the land and the sea, the Maori have passed down culinary methods, dishes, and seasonings that are still enjoyed today.

One Maori tradition that has become a favorite experience of visitors to New Zealand is hangi, a method of cooking using an earthen oven and heated rocks. This method of cooking can be found throughout the Pacific, and many variations can be made in order to achieve different results. First, a hole must be dug in the ground. The hole must be sheltered from wind and just big enough to fit the food to be heated and the hot stones. A fire is lit hours before the food is inserted, and wet cloth is used to create steam. The food (meat, then produce) is placed on the heated stones and covered. The dish is left to steam for a few hours depending on the size of the oven and the amount of food being prepared. In the past, this method would have been used to prepare fish and root vegetables. Today, hangi is used to cook pork, lamb, pumpkin, and a variety of other foods. Hangi is often reserved for special occasions, including Matariki, the Maori celebration of the New Year.

Another Maori culinary tradition that survives today is the making of *rewena*. *Rewena* is bread made from potatoes. It has a sweet and slightly sour taste as a result of the lengthy period of fermentation it undergoes. Most often compared to sourdough, *rewena* is found in many specialty bakeshops and markets in New Zealand.

Much of the plant life that was first harvested for use in Maori dishes is still being used in New Zealand dishes today. The leaves of both the horopito and kawakawa are ground or used as larger flakes and included in stuffing and marinades. *Pikopiko* (fern shoots) are peeled and rinsed to remove some of their bitterness. They can then be steamed, boiled, or stir-fried and added to dough or blended with oils and nuts.

NEW ZEALAND DESSERTS

No culinary region's identity would be complete without delicious desserts. Luckily, New Zealand has several sweet treats that are unique to Kiwis. From dishes named after Russian ballerinas to food for fairies, New Zealanders have their own spin on how to end a meal.

The New Zealand dessert with the most controversy surrounding it is probably the pavlova. This dish features a large meringue topped with cream and fresh fruit. Exactly when it was created and the true nationality of the pavlova's creator are up for debate, however, and therein lies the controversy. It is believed to have been created in honor of the Russian dancer Anna Pavlova during her tour through Australia or New Zealand, sometime during the 1920s. In 2008, Helen Leach's book *The Pavlova Story: A Slice of New Zealand's Culinary History* argued that the first known publication of the pavlova recipe occurred in New Zealand. Others have asserted that the dish originated in the United States, Australia, and Germany. In any case, New Zealanders enjoy the dessert year round but especially during the summer months and at Christmastime.

Fairy bread is a treat that satisfies younger New Zealanders. Made up of white bread that has been slathered with margarine or butter and covered with sprinkles, fairy bread is a favorite at children's birthday parties. While it is popular in New Zealand, it is also a favorite food of children in Australia.

Another New Zealand treat that appeals to both young and old Kiwis is hokey pokey. Hokey pokey is honeycomb toffee, which is often mixed in with vanilla ice cream.

Lolly cake is another treat that New Zealanders love. This confectionary dish features lollies, or candies. Traditional recipes include firm chewy marshmallows, which are chopped and added to a base mixture of butter, condensed milk, and malt biscuits. After mixing, it is rolled into a log shape and dusted with coconut. It is then refrigerated until it sets and is ready to be sliced and served. Lolly cakes can be found in Kiwi bakeries and grocery stores, but this is one of the few New Zealand traditions that is rarely available in foreign areas. Not even Australia, New Zealand's nearest neighbor, has embraced the lolly cake.

Kiwi kids love fairy bread, white bread slathered in margarine and covered in sprinkles.

BEVERAGES

While New Zealand lies a similar distance from the equator as the major wine-producing areas in Europe—from the Rhine Valley in the north, through Alsace, Champagne, Burgundy, Loire, and Bordeaux in France, and into southern Spain—its climatic conditions are quite different. The long, narrow shape of New Zealand's two main islands means that no location is more than 80 miles (129 km) from the sea, giving it a maritime climate.

Most of the vineyards lie in coastal areas, where they bask for an average of 2,200 sunshine hours each year and are cooled at night by sea breezes.

This climatic pattern provides ideal growing conditions, producing premium-quality grapes.

Wine making in New Zealand dates back to the earliest settlers. Pioneer missionary Samuel Marsden planted about one hundred vines at his mission station in Kerikeri, Bay of Islands, in 1819. When James Busby, British resident and a knowledgeable viticulturist (wine expert), arrived in 1833, he set about turning Marsden's grapes into wine.

Even the French navigator Dumont d'Urville was impressed with New Zealand wine, noting in his journal, "I was given a light white wine, very sparkling and delicious in taste, which I enjoyed very much."

The French Catholic missionary Bishop Pompallier also had an interest in wine, and he established another vineyard. During the next few years, grapevines were taken to other parts of New Zealand by French missionary priests.

New Zealand offers the perfect agricultural environment for vineyards, which have dotted the landscape for centuries.

Hardworking immigrants from Yugoslavia and Lebanon laid the foundations of the modern New Zealand commercial wine industry early in the twentieth century. But it was not until after World War II, when New Zealand servicemen returned from Europe having acquired a taste for European-style table wine, that winemakers in New Zealand had a local market.

Since the 1960s, there has continued to be rapid growth in wine production and consumption. Modern viticulturists have combined traditional vineyard practices with state-of-the-art techniques to enhance the flavor and produce wines with a distinctive New Zealand style. Today, New Zealand wine excites the world's judges and wine media commentators. In international competitions, New Zealand regularly wins high awards for its Sauvignon Blanc, Chardonnay, Cabernet/Merlot, and sparkling wines.

The British explorer James Cook pioneered brewing in New Zealand when he established a brewery at Dusty Sound. Today, there are several breweries in the country. New Zealand beer is similar to English- and Netherlands-style lagers, with Steinlager being one of the most popular beers, both in New Zealand and abroad.

INTERNET LINKS

http://www.newzealand.com/us/feature/favourite-new-zealand-foods
Visit this website to learn more about New Zealand's favorite foods.

https://www.youtube.com/watch?v=B8sKQeLmax0
Watch culinary tourists learn about traditional Maori foods and cooking methods.

WEST COAST WHITEBAIT PATTIES

Whitebait is a term for immature fish that are caught and fried. A delicacy in New Zealand, whitebait from the South Island's west coast is said to be the best. The best patties are the result of having less batter and more whitebait. Some New Zealanders also serve the young fry of fish with a mint sauce. If whitebait is not available, some suggest pieces of squid as an alternative.

3 eggs
½ cup milk
¾ cup flour
Salt and pepper to taste
1 tsp baking powder
1 pound whitebait
2 Tbsp light vegetable oil or 2 Tbsp butter (for frying)

DIRECTIONS
1. Beat the eggs in a large bowl, then mix in the milk.
2. Season with salt and pepper to taste.
3. Lightly beat through the flour and baking powder to ensure there are no lumps. Add the flour slowly—the mixture should be thick but not too gloopy.
4. In a colander, rinse the whitebait and pick out any river stones or other debris.
5. Drain, and mix into the egg mixture until well combined.
6. Heat a frying pan on medium-high heat, and once heated, add the butter/oil.
7. Drop in spoonfuls of the whitebait mixture, and cook until the patty is set (and starts to go golden on the underside). The whitebait will normally have gone white at this stage.
8. Turn, and cook on the other side until golden.
9. Keep warm in the oven until ready to serve.

AFGHAN BISCUIT

This chocolate and cornflake cookie is a national delight in New Zealand. These delicious treats are topped with chocolate icing and flaked almonds. Despite the dessert's name, it has no ties with Afghanistan. It is important to remember to use unsweetened cornflakes; otherwise the cookies will be too sweet.

14 Tbsp of butter, at room temperature
½ cup of castor sugar
1½ cups of all-purpose flour
3 Tbsp unsweetened cocoa powder
1½ cups of unsweetened cornflakes

To make the icing:
1 cup of icing sugar
2 Tbsp of unsweetened cocoa powder
3 Tbsp water
¼ cup of flaked almonds (optional)

DIRECTIONS
1. Preheat the oven to 350°F (180°C). Line a baking sheet with parchment paper.
2. Cream the butter and sugar until light and fluffy.
3. Sift together the flour and cocoa powder, and mix into butter mixture with a wooden spoon. Fold in cornflakes, and don't worry if they crumble.
4. Roll or press the dough into balls, each using 1½ teaspoons of dough, and flatten them slightly. Place them about 2 inches apart on the baking sheet.
5. Bake in the oven for 10 to 15 minutes. Remove from oven, and cool on a wire rack.
6. Prepare the icing by combining the icing sugar, unsweetened cocoa powder, and water in a bowl. Mix well until the mixture is free of lumps and is of a creamy consistency.
7. Spoon a little icing on each cookie, and decorate with flaked almonds.

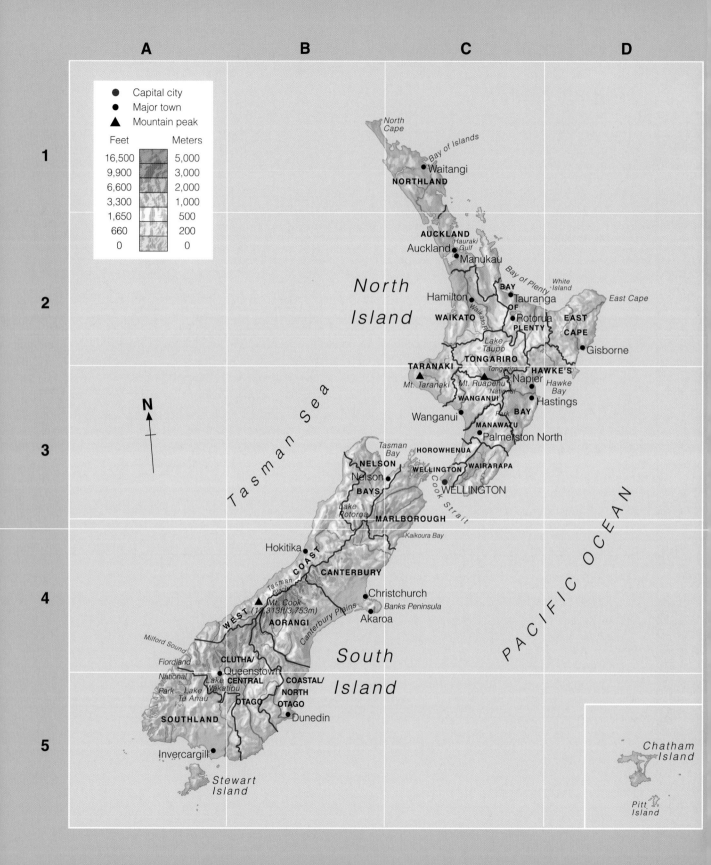

MAP OF NEW ZEALAND

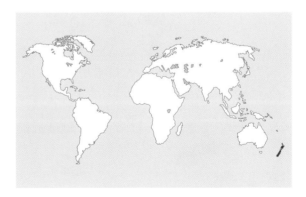

ECONOMIC NEW ZEALAND

Agriculture

- Dairy
- Fishing
- Forestry
- Wine

Natural Resources

- Gas
- Hydroelectric power
- Thermal power

Manufacturing

- Boat-building
- Communications
- Horse-breeding
- Oil
- Scientific/industrial

Services

- Airport
- Seaports
- Tourism

ABOUT THE ECONOMY

OVERVIEW

The economy of New Zealand previously relied greatly on international trade. However, in recent years, it has become more self-sufficient. Tourism rates have increased following successful campaigns and films set in the country. Agriculture and manufacturing, once heavily carrying the country, remain important to the economy. Economic free-market reforms over the last decades have removed many barriers to foreign investment. Internally, the country struggles with rising housing prices, making it difficult for people wishing to live in homes to own property. On an international level, New Zealand has free trade agreements with many countries, and it continues to seek other free trade agreements in the Pacific area.

GROSS DOMESTIC PRODUCT (GDP)

$185 billion (in US dollars) (2016 estimate)

GDP GROWTH

3.6 percent (2016 estimate)

CURRENCY

New Zealand dollar (NZD)
Notes: $5, $10, $20, $50, $100
Coins: 10 cents, 20 cents, 50 cents, $1, $2
1 USD = 1.37 NZD (September 2017)

NATURAL RESOURCES

Hydropower, coal, natural gas, oil, iron ore, sand, timber, gold, limestone

AGRICULTURAL PRODUCTS

Dairy products, sheep, beef, poultry, fruit, vegetables, wine, seafood, wheat, and barley

MAJOR EXPORTS

Dairy products, meat, wood and wood products, fruit, crude oil, wine

MAJOR IMPORTS

Petroleum, machinery, electrical equipment, vehicles and parts, textiles

MAIN TRADE PARTNERS

China, Australia, United States, Japan, Germany, Thailand, United Kingdom, and South Korea

WORKFORCE

2.598 million (2016 estimate)

UNEMPLOYMENT RATE

5.1 percent (2016 estimate)

INFLATION

0.6 percent (2016 estimate)

EXTERNAL DEBT

$81.39 billion (2016 estimate)

CULTURAL NEW ZEALAND

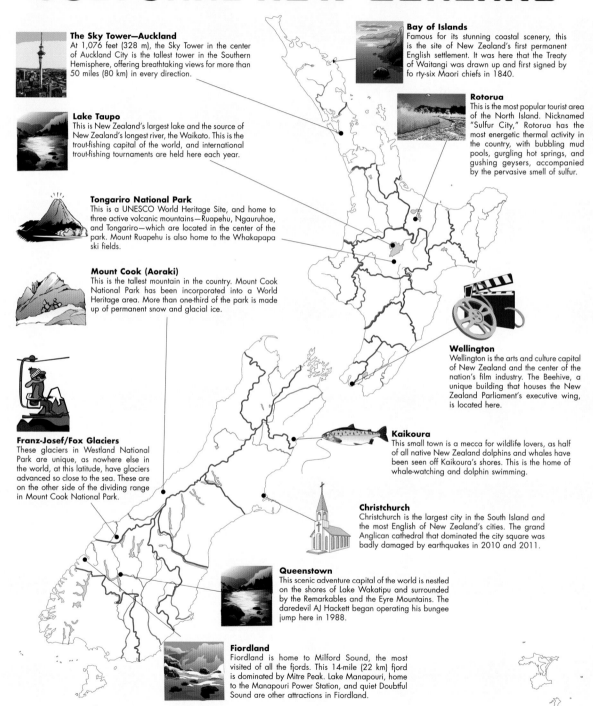

The Sky Tower—Auckland
At 1,076 feet (328 m), the Sky Tower in the center of Auckland City is the tallest tower in the Southern Hemisphere, offering breathtaking views for more than 50 miles (80 km) in every direction.

Lake Taupo
This is New Zealand's largest lake and the source of New Zealand's longest river, the Waikato. This is the trout-fishing capital of the world, and international trout-fishing tournaments are held here each year.

Tongariro National Park
This is a UNESCO World Heritage Site, and home to three active volcanic mountains—Ruapehu, Ngauruhoe, and Tongariro—which are located in the center of the park. Mount Ruapehu is also home to the Whakapapa ski fields.

Mount Cook (Aoraki)
This is the tallest mountain in the country. Mount Cook National Park has been incorporated into a World Heritage area. More than one-third of the park is made up of permanent snow and glacial ice.

Franz-Josef/Fox Glaciers
These glaciers in Westland National Park are unique, as nowhere else in the world, at this latitude, have glaciers advanced so close to the sea. These are on the other side of the dividing range in Mount Cook National Park.

Bay of Islands
Famous for its stunning coastal scenery, this is the site of New Zealand's first permanent English settlement. It was here that the Treaty of Waitangi was drawn up and first signed by forty-six Maori chiefs in 1840.

Rotorua
This is the most popular tourist area of the North Island. Nicknamed "Sulfur City," Rotorua has the most energetic thermal activity in the country, with bubbling mud pools, gurgling hot springs, and gushing geysers, accompanied by the pervasive smell of sulfur.

Wellington
Wellington is the arts and culture capital of New Zealand and the center of the nation's film industry. The Beehive, a unique building that houses the New Zealand Parliament's executive wing, is located here.

Kaikoura
This small town is a mecca for wildlife lovers, as half of all native New Zealand dolphins and whales have been seen off Kaikoura's shores. This is the home of whale-watching and dolphin swimming.

Christchurch
Christchurch is the largest city in the South Island and the most English of New Zealand's cities. The grand Anglican cathedral that dominated the city square was badly damaged by earthquakes in 2010 and 2011.

Queenstown
This scenic adventure capital of the world is nestled on the shores of Lake Wakatipu and surrounded by the Remarkables and the Eyre Mountains. The daredevil AJ Hackett began operating his bungee jump here in 1988.

Fiordland
Fiordland is home to Milford Sound, the most visited of all the fjords. This 14-mile (22 km) fjord is dominated by Mitre Peak. Lake Manapouri, home to the Manapouri Power Station, and quiet Doubtful Sound are other attractions in Fiordland.

ABOUT THE CULTURE

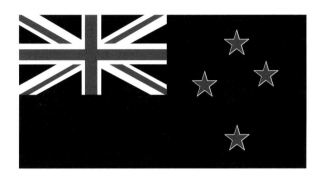

OFFICIAL NAME
New Zealand

FLAG DESCRIPTION
The New Zealand flag features, on a royal blue background, a Union Jack in the first quarter and four five-pointed red stars of the Southern Cross on the fly. The stars have white borders.

TOTAL AREA
103,799 square miles (268,838 sq km)

CAPITAL
Wellington

ETHNIC GROUPS
European and New Zealander 71.2 percent, Maori 14.1 percent, Asian 11.3 percent, Pacific Islander 7.6 percent, others 1.6 percent (2013 estimates)

RELIGION
Christianity (44.3 percent: Anglican 10.8 percent, Roman Catholic 11.6 percent, Presbyterian 7.8 percent, Methodist 2.4 percent, Pentecostal 1.8 percent), Hindu 2.1 percent, Buddhist 1.4 percent, Maori Christian 1.3, Islam 1.1 percent, no religion 38.5 percent (2013 estimate)

BIRTH RATE
13.2 births per 1,000 New Zealanders (2017 estimate)

DEATH RATE
7.5 deaths per 1,000 New Zealanders (2017 estimate)

MAIN LANGUAGES
English, Maori (official), New Zealand Sign Language (official)

TIMELINE

IN NEW ZEALAND	IN THE WORLD
circa 1200s CE Polynesian settlers, today known as the Maori, arrive in New Zealand.	
	1206–1368 CE Genghis Khan unifies the Mongols and starts conquest of the world.
	1517 Martin Luther launches the Protestant Reformation with his Ninety-Five Theses.
1642 Abel Tasman becomes the first European to sight New Zealand.	
1769 Captain James Cook explores the coasts of both the North and the South Islands of New Zealand. He returns in 1773 and 1777.	**1776** The United States declares independence from Britain.
1815 The first British missionaries arrive.	
1840 Treaty of Waitangi signed between the British and several Maori tribes.	**1837** The reign of Queen Victoria begins.
1845–1872 The New Zealand Wars, also referred to as the Land Wars, occur.	**1861** Czar Alexander II frees the serfs in Russia.
1893 New Zealand becomes the world's first nation to grant women the right to vote.	
1907 New Zealand becomes a dominion within the British Empire.	**1900** Hawaii becomes a US territory.
1914 Outbreak of World War I; New Zealand commits thousands of troops to the British war effort.	**1914–1918** World War I.
1939–1945 Troops from New Zealand see action in Europe, North Africa, and the Pacific during World War II.	**1939–1945** World War II.
1947 New Zealand gains full independence from Britain.	**1945** The United States drops atomic bombs on Hiroshima and Nagasaki.
	1949 The North Atlantic Treaty Organization (NATO) is formed.

IN NEW ZEALAND	IN THE WORLD
1984	
Labour Party government elected; Prime Minister David Lange begins radical economic reforms.	**1986** Nuclear power disaster at Chernobyl in Ukraine.
1989 Prime Minister Lange resigns, replaced by Geoffrey Palmer.	
1990 Palmer resigns just before the general election.	**1991** Breakup of the Soviet Union.
1993 National Party narrowly wins election; referendum introduces proportional representation.	
1997 After leadership challenge, Jim Bolger resigns and Jenny Shipley becomes first female prime minister.	**1997** Hong Kong is returned to China.
1999 The Labour Party wins election. Helen Clark becomes prime minister.	**2001** Terrorists crash planes in New York, Washington, DC, and Pennsylvania.
	2003 War in Iraq begins.
2005 Incumbent Prime Minister Helen Clark secures a narrow election win over the National Party.	
2008 John Key and National Party win victory in general election.	**2010** Arab Spring.
2011 Massive earthquake rocks Christchurch, killing almost two hundred people. All Blacks win Rugby World Cup.	**2011** Civil war breaks out in Syria.
2013 New Zealand becomes first country in Asia-Pacific to legalize gay marriage.	
2016 Prime Minister John Key resigns unexpectedly and Bill English is elected the new leader of the National Party.	**2016** Paris Climate Agreement is signed. Donald Trump is elected president of the United States.
2017 Jacinda Ardern is elected prime minister.	

GLOSSARY

Aorangi (ah-or-rung-ee)
"Cloud piercer"; Maori name for Mount Cook.

Aotearoa (ah-or-te-ah-roar)
"Land of the long white cloud"; Maori name for New Zealand.

haka (huh-kuh)
Energetic, aggressive action song traditionally performed by men; commonly performed today by the national rugby team, the All Blacks, before a match.

hangi (HAA-ngee)
An earth oven used by the Maori to cook food; today it also refers to the feast itself.

hapu (huh-POO)
A subtribe.

hui (hoo-ee)
Maori social and political gathering to which Europeans may be invited.

iwi (ee-wee)
A tribe.

karanga (kah-rah-ngah)
A call to visitors (always made by a woman) to enter the meetinghouse; the *karanga* is returned by a female leader on behalf of the visitors.

kumara (KOO-mah-rah)
Sweet potato.

mana (mah-nah)
Prestige, status, or honor.

marae (mah-rye)
A social place where religious and secular activities take place; a rural Maori concept that has also been established in the cities.

pa (PAA)
An earthwork fort commonly built by pre-European Maori.

pakeha (PAA-ke-haa)
A Maori term for the European settlers in New Zealand.

poi (poy)
Small balls on the ends of strings used by female Maori performers.

pyroclastic
Rocks that are formed as a result of volcanic ash.

tapu (tuh-poo)
Maori word associated with Maori spiritual beliefs, meaning "sacred" or "holy."

whanau (FAA-no-oo)
Extended family.

FOR FURTHER INFORMATION

BOOKS

Buerger, Dianne, and Zuraidah Omar, eds. *DK Eyewitness Travel: New Zealand*. New York: DK Eyewitness, 2016.

Colson, Mary. *New Zealand*. Countries Around the World. Chicago, IL: Heinemann, 2012.

Larson, Lyn. *New Zealand*. Country Explorers. Minneapolis, MN: Lerner, 2011.

Ortolja-Baird, Ljiljana. *New Zealand: Culture Smart!: The Essential Guide to Customs and Culture*. London, UK: Kuperard, 2017.

Rawlings-Way, Charles, et. al. *New Zealand*. Melbourne, Australia: Lonely Planet, 2016.

WEBSITES

CIA World Factbook, https://www.cia.gov/library/publications/the-world-factbook/geos/nz.html.

Lonely Planet, https://www.lonelyplanet.com/new-zealand.

NewsHub, http://www.newshub.co.nz/home.html.

New Zealand Government, https://www.govt.nz.

Radio NZ, http://www.radionz.co.nz.

FILM

Lord of the Rings trilogy. DVD. New Line Cinemas, 2001—2003.

New Zealand to the Max. DVD. American Public Television, 2007.

The Ultimate New Zealand. DVD. Custom Flix, 2006.

The Whale Rider. DVD. Pandora Film. 2002.

MUSIC

Kiri Te Kanawa: Maori Songs. EMI Classics, 1999.

Te Runga Rawa: New Zealand: Maoris Songs. Playsound, 2007.

Various Artists: Songs of New Zealand. MasterSound, 2000.

BIBLIOGRAPHY

Balham, Diana, and Kate Fraser. *Frommer's New Zealand*. New York: Frommer Media LLC, 2017.

Belton, Rosie, and Margaret Mahy. *Wild Blackberries: Recipes and Memories from a New Zealand Table*. Sydney, Australia: Allen & Unwin, 2014.

Bennett, Joe. *A Land of Two Halves: An Accidental Tour of New Zealand*. London, UK: Scribner, 2005.

Darby, Anabel. *Fodor's Essential New Zealand*. New York: Fodor's Travel Publications, 2017.

Elliott, Matt. *War Blacks: The Extraordinary Story of New Zealand's World War I All Blacks*. London, UK: HarperCollins, 2016.

Emmler, Clemens, and Klaus Viedebantt. *New Zealand: Continent in a Nutshell*. New York: Bucher, 2007.

English, Tom, and Peter Burns. *When Lions Roared: The Lions, the All Blacks and the Legendary Tour of 1971*. Sweden: Polaris, 2017.

Evans, Polly. *Kiwis Might Fly: Around New Zealand on Two Big Wheels*. New York: Bantam, 2010.

Fischer, David Hackett. *Fairness and Freedom: A History of Two Open Societies*. New York: Oxford University Press, 2012.

Loveridge, Steven. *New Zealand Society at War*. Chicago: IPG-Academic, 2017.

Masson, J. Moussaieff. *Slipping into Paradise: Why I Live in New Zealand*. New York: Ballantine, 2005.

McLauchlan, Gordon. *A Short History of New Zealand*. Auckland, New Zealand: David Bateman, 2014.

Smith, Philippa Mein. *A Concise History of New Zealand*. Cambridge, UK: Cambridge University Press, 2012.

INDEX

INDEX